Harmony is the Healer

Ingrid S. Kraaz von Rohr is a naturopath, classical homoeopath and colour therapist with her own practice near Munich. For many years she has specialized in work with healing vibrations. She was for several years responsible to the Fachverband der Deutschen Heilpraktiker (the Professional Association of German Naturopaths) for the direction of all specialized training in the Munich area. She also founded the International Academy of Complementary Medicine, Santa Fe, New Mexico, and Grünwald near Munich.

Wulfing von Rohr was the original discoverer and publisher of Dr Edward Bach in Germany. He is a television journalist and producer, and the author of books on a variety of subjects. He wrote *Meditation – Energy from Within*, and also co-authored Chris Griscom's two successful books *The Healing of Emotion* and *Time is an Illusion*, as well as Annelise Harf's *Yoga – Weg zur Harmonie*.

Harmony is the Healer

The combined handbook to
healing flowers, colour therapy,
Schüssler tissue-salts, emergency homoeopathy
and other forms of vibrational medicine

BY INGRID AND WULFING VON ROHR

Translated from the German by
Peter Lemesurier

ELEMENT
Shaftesbury, Dorset ● Rockport, Massachusetts
Brisbane, Queensland

© Wilhelm Goldmann Verlag, München 1989
English translation © Peter Lemesurier 1992

Published in Great Britain in 1992 by
Element Books Limited
Longmead, Shaftesbury, Dorset

Published in the USA in 1992 by
Element, Inc
42 Broadway, Rockport, MA 01966

Published in Australia in 1992 by
Element Books Limited for
Jacaranda Wiley Limited
33 Park Road, Milton, Brisbane 4064

Cover design by Barbara McGavin
Text illustrations by Fritz Urich (pp. 35, 56, 59)
and Cindy Schroeder
Designed by Roger Lightfoot
Typeset by Footnote Graphics, Warminster, Wiltshire
Printed and bound in Great Britain by
Dotesios Ltd, Trowbridge, Wiltshire

CIP data available
Library of Congress Data available

ISBN 1-85230-242-9

'It says in the scriptures that we are made of body, mind and soul! We have made wonderful progress in developing our body and intellect, but unfortunately we have neglected the soul. Our soul is a drop in the ocean of cosmic consciousness. Therefore its true nature is light, life and love.'

Sant Darshan Singh (1921–1989)

Contents

Translator's foreword

The field of 'energy medicine' or 'vibrational medicine' is fraught with linguistic and conceptual vagueness. Uncertainty reigns over precisely what it is about healing flower essences, colour therapy, Schüssler tissue-salts or homoeopathic remedies that actually does the healing. The mechanics of the healing process remain ill-defined, largely unresearched and hence for the most part impossible to put into words. How, then, to describe the indescribable? The original German title of this book, frequently recalled in the text, is *Die richtige Schwingung heilt*. But translating the idea is far from straightforward. German words do not mean English words, and consequently *Schwingung*, especially as used here by the authors, has no single equivalent in English.

What heals, it would seem, is the 'right vibration', the 'right frequency', the 'right resonance'. Health is a subtle level of harmonious activity within the human organism, and re-activating it by whatever means is thus the key to healing. In this way symptoms, far from being directly combated, are simply made superfluous.

This, then, is the theme that constantly informs the book. Readers may debate the how and why. But that healing can result from applying the particular therapies described is a fact that the authors claim to have demonstrated repeatedly in their own healing work, and this book represents their attempt to harmonize them into a new, do-it-yourself, 'multi-energy' approach that is both practical and uniquely comprehensive.

Acknowledgements

It has become my life's work to share with others the ideas of my favourite philosopher Plato, as well as other forms of practical philosophy that are of relevance to modern times. Plato's basic insights – such as his recognition that 'The soul heals the body' – are for me supreme examples of sanity and reason. I have always been similarly impressed by Goethe, and particularly by his theory of colour.

From both I have gained the fundamental insight that, right from the very conception of creation, human beings have been destined to live in conscious harmony with creation itself.

Like a good many of the world's healers, I also owe the basis of such healing skills as I have to two other great thinkers – namely Samuel Hahnemann, founder of homoeopathy, and Dr Edward Bach, the discoverer of a new method of healing whose significance many practitioners believe to be on a par with homoeopathy. In fact my own experience suggests that the two therapeutic approaches actually complement each other.

What knowledge and wisdom Hahnemann and Bach still have to offer us today! Without their fascinating findings we should be hard put to it to diagnose and balance the various vibrationary disharmonies between soul and personality, or between body, mind and soul.

I should like to express special thanks to Josef Angerer, doyen of naturopathy in Germany and founder of the healers' vocational college in Munich. Equally I wish to thank Peter Mandel, through whom I first gained practical access to the world of resonances and vibrations. A grateful acknowledgement goes to Ian Miller and The

C. W. Daniel Company Ltd for publishing Dr Edward Bach's works for so long and so well.

I gratefully acknowledge the mental and spiritual guidance of my spiritual master Sant Darshan Singh, as well as of my beloved Saint-Germain, both of whom have inspired me and awakened my understanding of higher-dimensional powers and principles.

Last but not least, we should both like to thank Johannes Jacob for his personal commitment to promoting and supporting a handbook such as this, dealing as it does with harmonious vibrations as the essential basis of all health, and, of course, Michael Mann and his wonderful team at Element Books, who have undertaken to publish the book in English, and Peter Lemesurier, who has translated our handbook with such rare and subtle understanding.

Finally we would recall two thoughts of Goethe – first, that there is no universal truth, but that every truth has its own individual tinge; and secondly, that research into the hidden aspects of life is not the prerogative of any single generation. In this sense the present book is but a step along the way, and in no way to be seen as the ultimate goal itself.

Ingrid von Rohr

Introduction

HEALTH PROMOTION IN PLACE OF
DISEASE-ORIENTED THINKING

The right
vibration heals
'The doctor knows best.' This simple piece of folk wisdom reflects most people's attitude to medicine. Ours has been a period when new scientific discoveries have been translated into such medical breakthroughs as the use of penicillin and the development of modern surgical techniques. But this period has also been marked increasingly by a drift towards a technocratic form of medical practice based on sheer gadgetry – and one that has lost sight of the human being as a whole entity made up of body, mind and spirit.

Symptomatic of this attitude is a remark dating from 1988 made by a professorial colleague in the West German health ministry, to the effect that any medicine has to prove its effectiveness in the context of the sick-bed. As if there were not plenty of medicines to help people *steer clear* of the sick-bed! And as if, too, sensible precautions and early diagnosis were not at least as important as treating diseases that have already reached such an advanced stage as to make the sick-bed unavoidable!

Our thinking is largely disease-based, rather than concerned with health promotion. Even our use of such 'positive' terms as 'health services', 'health insurance' and 'health food' cannot disguise the fact. Over the years disease has grown into a political and economic problem of the first order. Grandiose thinking and the shameless exploitation of our health – through bad diet and health-damaging environmental influences, as well as through a symptom-obsessed and physically oriented form of medicine – have brought about a state of affairs where what is in fact our *sickness* service is in the process of outstripping our means.

It is high time, then, that we had a real *health* service, together with genuine *health* provision, *health* support and so on. But all this has to be based on the right mental attitude and a holistic view both of people and of the world they live in, as well as on our learning to understand the subtle and complex interactions between the spiritual, psycho-emotional and physical processes that are all at work within the human organism.

In the field of health this insight has long been the very foundation on which healers, naturopaths, homoeopaths and enlightened doctors have based their diagnostic and therapeutic work.

The threat to 'natural' medicine Natural medicine (ever since Paracelsus) and homoeopathy (ever since Hahnemann) constitute an important and widely recognized aspect of health-care. A more recent tendency, however, encouraged by politicians and the representatives of authority and industry, is to take the line that existing unorthodox therapies and remedies should be restricted, displaced by means of market pressure or even made illegal. No less than 2,500 tried and tested preparations and substances are set to disappear if certain authorities have their way.

One can imagine what an outcry such people would raise if naturopaths and other responsible citizens were to demand that smoking be officially banned throughout the country and subjected to penalties. And this despite the fact that the dangers of smoking have long since been demonstrated even by orthodox medicine. Yet effective natural remedies are, it seems, to be abolished as an alleged risk to public health!

Therapeutic freedom In the process, our so-called therapeutic liberty – the freedom of each one of us to decide what is good for us, which is something that we ourselves are inherently far better at than the representatives of any interest or lobby – is undermined, if not finally removed.

All the more significant, then, are the constructive efforts that are currently being made to develop, test and promote holistic medical approaches. In the process, those approaches that see the human being as an 'energy system' are increasingly taking up centre-stage. The latest buzzwords in this area are 'healing flower essences', 'colour therapy' and 'Kirlian photography' – not to mention 'meditation'. These represent the continuation of a tradition whose origins lie centuries and even millennia ago in acupuncture, homoeopathy, herbalism and the like.

Why should it not be possible, then, for all these differing viewpoints and therapeutic approaches to come together to form a sensible whole – to the greater benefit of humanity at large?

Is a coming together of university teachers, orthodox medics and the representatives of political and industrial interests on the one hand and naturopaths, healers, private researchers and spiritually-minded people on the other still seemingly so out of the question, so blocked by considerations of status and supposed superiority, that next to nothing can be done? East and West can come together, there is talk of disarmament, confidence-building measures and co-operation, weapons are being scrapped, yet within our health services what reigns among the establishment is predominantly hostility, or at best non-communication – to the detriment of the vast majority of patients.

In British hospitals it is not unusual for so-called spiritual healers to be allowed to practise alongside the normal therapies – and very successful they often are too. A recent study in the USA has shown that patients who are prayed for get better faster than those who are not. In 1988 a French doctor finally succeeded in demonstrating that homoeopathic remedies which no longer contain even a single molecule of the 'potentized' substance are still effective, apparently as a result of 'bio-information' imprinted on the very water involved. And Canadian and Israeli institutes have since confirmed these experimental results.

Quite often, nevertheless, the representatives of established and largely economic interests go out of their way to avoid any even-handed dialogue. Even communications between holistic doctors, homoeopaths and healers of various ilks and orientations still leave much to be desired. Everybody seems to forget that for patients – for individual people – the restoration and maintenance of health is far more important than mere theoretical arguments.

Health is not a commodity

People need to become more aware of the fact that every individual bears responsibility for his or her own health. Health is not a commodity to be bought. On the other hand it is also true that the therapist's state of consciousness has a large bearing on assessing both the treatment and its degree of 'success'.

It is in this spirit that the present handbook offers both basic introductions to, and practical advice and guidance on, a variety of major natural therapies. It is intended both for healers and for ordinary people who would simply like to do something positive about their own health. It is a handbook designed to build bridges, to point up fruitful complementarities, to indicate sensible ways in which a whole variety of modes of healing can be combined with one another.

'The doctor knows best.' As the authors of this book, we would amend this piece of folklore to read, 'What is best is what works *for the individual person concerned.*'

One of the most exciting rediscoveries of our time in the therapeutic field is the recognition that health represents a quite specific state of harmonic resonance, and that it is a falling away from this harmony that we experience as 'illness'. If health is a harmonious vibration and illness a discordant one, then it is possible to restore the human condition from a state of 'illness' to one of 'health' simply by means of the right resonances.

Harmony is the healer: the right vibration heals!

Life is vibration Everything in life – indeed, in the whole gamut of creation – is created and permeated by energy-vibrations. It is via these energy-vibrations that everything in creation stands in a more or less intimate relationship to everything else.

Every stone, every plant, every animal, every human being – all have their own form of vibration. All forms of natural energy, all forms of radiation (such as light, heat and so on), all colours and all forms of information are essentially vibrations. Music is widely recognized as taking the form of vibrations which can have harmonious or disharmonious effects. Thoughts, too, are vibrations that can equally well have harmonious or disharmonious effects.

Opportunities and tasks

It is both our opportunity and our task as human beings:

1. To make ourselves aware of the nature and character of the vibrations and energies that
   - influence us,
   - work on us from the past through our heredity and conditioning,
   - surround our personality,
   - are finally brought by us into full expression;
2. To recognize just how we react on the purely physical and 'automatic' level both to external influences (including electromagnetic environmental pollution!) and to internal impulses;
3. To become aware of what vibrations are emanating *from our souls*;
4. To take full responsibility for our every thought and word, since these transmit tangible energies of their own;
5. And finally to come to the realization that all powers, energies and vibrations have their origin in the spiritual realm.

The effects of thought

Once we realize how influential thoughts and words can be – whether for good or ill – we can more readily accept that every thought that we harbour, articulate or write down contains its own force which then begins to radiate outwards. How quickly other people's faces change, after all, the moment they hear from us either friendly words or angry and dismissive ones!

Try it some time: when somebody near to you has a difficult interview to face, tell them that you will be thinking positively about them and their situation at the time. This is something that has been tried many times – and it works!

Illness is nothing but a breakdown in harmonious vibrations, or an emanation of disharmonious vibrations that have first been experienced on the inner levels. Three historical quotations express the point in exemplary fashion:

'It is spirit that builds the body.' (Schiller)
'The soul heals the body.' (Plato)
'The spirit within us is the only all-powerful doctor, and the only true panacea is to submit oneself to it.' (Sri Aurobindo)

1. The healing flower essences

The revolutionary discoveries of Dr Edward Bach

Edward Bach* was born the son of a brass-founder near Birmingham, England in 1886. At the age of sixteen he entered his father's firm. In the meantime he felt inwardly called to healing, and between 1906 and 1913 studied orthodox medicine as currently taught at London University. Subsequently he devoted himself with distinction to general practice, spending several years in London's famous Harley Street, before taking on the additional post of pathologist and bacteriologist at the London Homoeopathic Hospital.

Edward Bach soon became disillusioned by the limited healing success of the purely 'academic' therapies and, driven by his own experiences of grave illness as well as by an overflowing love for suffering co-humanity, he set out to find new avenues of healing.

The starting point for his later, pioneering discovery of the effectiveness of flower essences was his own research into, and therapeutic application of, so-called intestinal 'nosodes' (special medicaments produced by the homoeopathic potentization of disease particles: see also page [9]. Edward Bach started by establishing that a whole series of illnesses, and particularly certain chronic complaints, could be most effectively treated by detoxifying the intestinal tract.

In the course of his work he discovered that seven major groups of bacteria corresponded to seven major groups of mind-states. Edward Bach realized that these respective states of mind apparently had something to do with the diseases people suffer from, and so some direct, if as yet indeterminate, connection must exist between psychological sensations and physical symptoms. But this

*Pronounced 'Batch' – Tr.

was an unfamiliar notion to the 'modern', scientifically-trained doctors of his time, with their exaggerated faith in materialism.

On the basis of these seven groups of bacteria he developed seven 'Bach nosodes', and with them was able to achieve some extraordinarily impressive results. Nevertheless, even these successes did not satisfy him, as he wanted to be able to heal not just one particular type of illness, but as many as possible, if not all diseases whatever.

Edward Bach now went on to search for natural, God-given remedies that did not need to be produced in the same expensive, synthetic way as his nosodes. In 1928 he discovered the first three of the thirty-eight flower remedies that were subsequently to replace his 'Bach nosodes'.

At the beginning of 1930 Edward Bach decided to turn his back on London and to settle down in the Welsh countryside. He felt himself driven to give up his lucrative practice and the international attention that his laboratory work in London was attracting, in favour of research work of a kind which was to expose him more and more to criticism by the medical establishment.

Flower-dew healing
By dint of numerous experiments on himself, as well as through inspiration from higher sources, Edward Bach discovered first twelve, then eventually thirty-eight flowers and plants to be particularly effective as remedies. He assumed that the healing vibration of each particular flower or plant must be conserved in its pure, concentrated form in the flower-dew itself.

His female collaborator, Nora Weeks, who like him has since died, quotes him as saying that the earth is the ground which bears and supports the plants; the air is what nourishes them; the sun or the fire enables them to transfer their energy; and the water finally takes up their beneficent healing powers and stores them.

Edward Bach developed a 'solar method', to all intents and purposes a new procedure for potentization, by which the fresh flowers could transfer their healing vibrations to water without being destroyed in the process.

So it was that he finally turned his back on orthodox medicine, refusing to be diverted by the authorities, despite their threats to withdraw his credentials, from teaching sufferers and non-sufferers alike about the positive effects of particular plants, while encouraging patients to heal themselves and at the same time training healers in his methods.

Edward Bach's most revolutionary realization – apart from his discovery of the seven main types of mind-state and the way in which the healing powers of plants could be transferred to water – is without doubt the insight that every disease is the physically tangible, visible and perceptible result of a discordant vibration that has already long since arisen within the personality itself.

His credo could thus be summarized as follows:

Edward Bach's findings The potential nature of humanity is total harmony between God (or the Creative Power), the soul (which is of the same essence as the Creative Power) and the individual personality. If this harmony is disturbed by the 'ego' on the personality-level, illness can arise. Such negative, disease-producing vibrations can best be dissolved on the inner level by the healing vibrations of particular flowers and plants. Recovery then follows.

In this way the soul opens itself to the Creative Power and so receives inner guidance as to how life is to be lived. The soul endeavours to pass this guidance on to the individual personality. Too often, however, the personality (the 'ego') is not prepared to trust itself to the soul's guidance. Discord between personality and soul then follows. This vibratory disharmony continually increases in intensity if it is not dissolved, and finally leads to illness of body and mind.

The healing vibrations of particular flowers and plants bring about or promote recovery by harmonizing the subtle, inner levels of the mind – at the very 'cutting edge' between, on the one hand, ego, mind, personality and so on and, on the other hand, the soul.

All great thoughts are simple 'All great thoughts are simple.' As though to prove this insight Edward Bach discovered that seven major groups of discordant vibrations are ultimately responsible for all illnesses – namely fear, uncertainty, insufficient interest in present circumstances, loneliness, over-sensitivity, despondency or despair and excessive concern for the welfare of others.

When he died in 1936, Edward Bach left behind him a hitherto totally unknown therapeutic approach which, as a result of countless positive experiences, is nowadays constantly growing in significance.

In this handbook we reproduce Dr Bach's therapeutic approach faithfully and in detail. At the same time we present for the first time a systematic correlation of the seven Bach groups and the thirty-eight healing flower essences with other, equally significant therapies, showing how their influences can be combined.

Healing flower therapy is based on the effectiveness of subtle vibrations, just as are colour therapy, emergency homoeopathy, the use of Schüssler's twelve mineral or tissue-salts and, last but by no means least, meditation and affirmation.

Our view is that healers should seek out some sensible way of applying tried and tested therapies of all kinds *in combination*, without dogmatically treating any one of them as superior. 'The right vibration heals', and complementary vibrations that operate on a variety of levels within body, mind and soul can all operate to their common advantage.

On the following pages the healing flower therapy is described first, followed by the other modes of healing and their various interrelationships.

The seven types of disharmony

Edward Bach had recognized that seven fundamental kinds of disturbance to the harmony of the personality are the cause of all disease symptoms. In his booklet *The Twelve Healers and Other Remedies* he specifically assigned the thirty-eight flower essences that he had discovered to seven such groups.

As his introduction puts it, 'No science, no knowledge is necessary, apart from the simple methods described herein.'

We interpret this to mean that there is no need to seek out further flower essences in addition to his original thirty-eight, and that his own descriptions and classifications of the thirty-eight remedies are quite sufficient in themselves. Nevertheless this does not exclude the possibility of bringing in other tried and tested natural therapies to complement and reinforce Edward Bach's method of healing, with its use of subtle, intangible vibrations to bring about inner harmony. No responsible natural healer would rule out additional forms of diagnosis and therapy and insist on applying one single, inflexible approach only.

Seven personality types

A division into seven groups was something that Edward Bach had already undertaken. As we pointed out previously, he started out his developmental and healing work with seven intestinal nosodes. The basis for this was his discovery that the toxins produced by certain bacteria within the human gut brought about chronic illnesses. Once the toxins were removed, the troubles disappeared. He therefore developed vaccines and nosodes against these intestinal bacteria. Yet his eventual aim was to replace both vaccines and nosodes with pure remedies drawn from nature.

He divided patients into seven distinct personality types with seven clearly identifiable character structures and symptomatic states of mind.

We see no reason to abandon this division into seven main groups, as many authors tend to do today. We believe that we should stick to Edward Bach's own well-established findings in our descriptions of the various states of mind, symptoms and treatment areas, while still leaving readers free to work out for themselves any further interpretations they please.

These seven groups are:
1. Fear
2. Uncertainty
3. Insufficient interest in present circumstances
4. Loneliness
5. Over-sensitivity to influences and ideas
6. Despondency or despair
7. Over-care for the welfare of others

Edward Bach's basic maxim

Edward Bach's basic healing maxim was: 'Take no notice of the disease, think only of the outlook on life of the one in distress.'

There follow descriptions, in Bach's own words, of the thirty-eight flower essences. (The figure in brackets after each name reflects the number – from 1 to 38 – assigned to it by Edward Bach.) On pages [23–5] will be found a summary designed to facilitate speedy reference to the

remedies, whether in terms of the seven groups, alpha-
betically or by number.

1. *For those who*   **Rock Rose (26)**
have fear   The *remedy of emergency* for cases where there even
appears no hope. In accident or sudden illness, or when
the patient is very frightened or terrified, or if the condition is serious enough to cause great fear to those around.
If the patient is not conscious the lips may be moistened
with the remedy. Other remedies in addition may also be
required, as, for example, if there is unconsciousness,
which is a deep, sleepy state, Clematis (9); if there is
torture, Agrimony (1) and so on.

Mimulus (20)
Fear of worldly things, illness, pain, accidents, poverty, of
dark, of being alone, of misfortune. The fears of everyday
life. These people quietly and secretly bear their dread,
they do not freely speak of it to others.

Cherry Plum (6)
Fear of the mind being over-strained, of reason giving
way, of doing fearful and dreaded things, not wished and
known wrong, yet there comes the thought and impulse
to do them.

Aspen (2)
Vague unknown fears, for which there can be given no
explanation, no reason.
    Yet the patient may be terrified of something terrible
going to happen, he knows not what.
    These vague unexplainable fears may haunt by night or
day.
    Sufferers are often afraid to tell their trouble to others.

Red Chestnut (25)
For those who find it difficult not to be anxious for other
people.
    Often they have ceased to worry about themselves, but
for those of whom they are fond they may suffer much,
frequently anticipating that some unfortunate thing may
happen to them.

2. For those who
suffer uncertainty

Cerato (5)
Those who have not sufficient confidence in themselves to make their own decisions.

They constantly seek advice from others, and are often misguided.

Scleranthus (28)
Those who suffer much from being unable to decide between two things, first one seeming right then the other.

They are usually quiet people, and bear their difficulty alone, as they are not inclined to discuss it with others.

Gentian (12)
Those who are easily discouraged. They may be progressing well in illness or in the affairs of their daily life, but any small delay or hindrance to progress causes doubt and soon disheartens them.

Gorse (13)
Very great hopelessness, they have given up belief that more can be done for them.

Under persuasion or to please others they may try different treatments, at the same time assuring those around that there is so little hope of relief.

Hornbeam (17)
For those who feel that they have not sufficient strength, mentally or physically, to carry the burden of life placed upon them; the affairs of every day seem too much for them to accomplish, though they generally succeed in fulfilling their task.

For those who believe that some part, of mind or body, needs to be strengthened before they can easily fulfil their work.

Wild Oat (36)
Those who have ambitions to do something of prominence in life, who wish to have much experience, and to enjoy all that which is possible for them, to take life to the full.

Their difficulty is to determine what occupation to follow; as although their ambitions are strong, they have no calling which appeals to them above all others.

This may cause delay and dissatisfaction.

3. Not sufficient interest in present circumstances

Clematis (9)
Those who are dreamy, drowsy, not fully awake, no great interest in life. Quiet people, not really happy in their present circumstances, living more in the future than in the present; living in hopes of happier times, when their ideals may come true. In illness some make little or no effort to get well, and in certain cases may even look forward to death, in the hope of better times; or maybe, meeting again some beloved one whom they have lost.

Honeysuckle (16)
Those who live much in the past, perhaps a time of great happiness, or memories of a lost friend, or ambitions which have not come true. They do not expect further happiness such as they have had.

Wild Rose (37)
Those who without apparently sufficient reason become resigned to all that happens, and just glide through life, take it as it is, without any effort to improve things and find some joy. They have surrendered to the struggle of life without complaint.

Olive (23)
Those who have suffered much mentally or physically and are so exhausted and weary that they feel they have no more strength to make any effort. Daily life is hard work for them, without pleasure.

White Chestnut (35)
For those who cannot prevent thoughts, ideas, arguments which they do not desire from entering their minds. Usually at such times when the interest of the moment is not strong enough to keep the mind full.

Thoughts which worry and will remain, or if for a time thrown out, will return. They seem to circle round and round and cause mental torture.

The presence of such unpleasant thoughts drives out peace and interferes with being able to think only of the work or pleasure of the day.

Mustard (21)
Those who are liable to times of gloom, or even despair, as though a cold dark cloud overshadowed them and hid

the light and the joy of life. It may not be possible to give any reason or explanation for such attacks.

Under these conditions it is almost impossible to appear happy or cheerful.

Chestnut Bud (7)

For those who do not take full advantage of observation and experience, and who take a longer time than others to learn the lessons of daily life.

Whereas one experience would be enough for some, such people find it necessary to have more, sometimes several, before the lesson is learnt.

Therefore, to their regret, they find themselves having to make the same error on different occasions when once would have been enough, or observation of others could have spared them even that one fault.

4. Loneliness

Water Violet (34)

For those who in health or illness like to be alone. Very quiet people, who move about without noise, speak little, and then gently. Very independent, capable and self-reliant. Almost free of the opinions of others. They are aloof, leave people alone and go their own way. Often clever and talented. Their peace and calmness is a blessing to those around them.

Impatiens (18)

Those who are quick in thought and action and who wish all things to be done without hesitation or delay. When ill they are anxious for a hasty recovery.

They find it very difficult to be patient with people who are slow, as they consider it wrong and a waste of time, and they will endeavour to make such people quicker in all ways.

They often prefer to work and think alone, so that they can do everything at their own speed.

Heather (14)

Those who are always seeking the companionship of anyone who may be available, as they find it necessary to discuss their own affairs with others, no matter whom it may be. They are very unhappy if they have to be alone for any length of time.

5. *Over-sensitive* **Agrimony (1)**
to influences and The jovial, cheerful, humorous people who love peace
ideas and are distressed by argument or quarrel, to avoid which
they will agree to give up much.

    Though generally they have troubles and are tormented
and restless and worried in mind or in body, they hide
their cares behind their humour and jesting and are considered very good friends to know. They often take
alcohol or drugs in excess, to stimulate themselves and
help themselves bear their trials with cheerfulness.

Centaury (4)
Kind, quiet, gentle people who are over-anxious to serve
others. They overtax their strength in their endeavours.

    Their wish so grows upon them that they become more
servants than willing helpers. Their good nature leads
them to do more than their own share of work, and in so
doing they may neglect their own particular mission in
life.

Walnut (33)
For those who have definite ideals and ambitions in life
and are fulfilling them, but on rare occasions are tempted
to be led away from their own ideas, aims and work by
the enthusiasm, convictions or strong opinions of others.

    The remedy gives constancy and protection from out-
side influences.

Holly (15)
For those who are sometimes attacked by thoughts of
such kind as jealousy, envy, revenge, suspicion.

    For the different forms of vexation.

    Within themselves they may suffer much, often when
there is no real cause for their unhappiness.

6. *For* **Larch (19)**
despondency or For those who do not consider themselves as good or
despair capable as those around them, who expect failure, who
feel that they will never be a success, and so do not
venture or make a strong enough attempt to succeed.

Pine (24)
For those who blame themselves. Even when successful
they think they could have done better, and are never

content with their efforts or the results. They are hard-working and suffer much from the faults they attach to themselves.

Sometimes if there is any mistake it is due to another, but they will claim responsibility even for that.

Elm (11)
Those who are doing good work, are following the calling of their life and who hope to do something of importance, and this often for the benefit of humanity.

At times there may be periods of depression when they feel that the task they have undertaken is too difficult, and not within the power of a human being.

Sweet Chestnut (30)
For those moments which happen to some people when the anguish is so great as to seem to be unbearable.

When the mind or body feels as if it had borne to the uttermost limit of its endurance, and that now it must give way.

When it seems there is nothing but destruction and annihilation left to face.

Star of Bethlehem (29)
For those in great distress under conditions which for a time produce great unhappiness.

The shock of serious news, the loss of someone dear, the fright following an accident, and such like.

For those who for a time refuse to be consoled, this remedy brings comfort.

Willow (38)
For those who have suffered adversity or misfortune and find these difficult to accept, without complaint or resentment, as they judge life much by the success which it brings.

They feel that they have not deserved so great a trial, that it was unjust, and they become embittered.

They often take less interest and are less active in those things of life which they had previously enjoyed.

Oak (22)
For those who are struggling and fighting strongly to get well, or in connection with the affairs of their daily life.

They will go on trying one thing after another though their case may seem hopeless.

They will fight on. They are discontented with themselves if illness interferes with their duties or helping others.

They are brave people, fighting against great difficulties, without loss of hope or effort.

Crab Apple (10)
This is the *remedy of cleansing.*

For those who feel as if they had something not quite clean about themselves.

Often it is something of apparently little importance; in others there may be more serious disease which is almost disregarded compared to the one thing on which they concentrate.

In both types they are anxious to be free from the one particular thing which is greatest in their minds and which seems so essential to them that it should be cured.

They become despondent if treatment fails.

Being a cleanser, this remedy purifies wounds if the patient has reason to believe that some poison has entered which must be drawn out.

7. Over-care for welfare of others

Chicory (8)
Those who are very mindful of the needs of others. They tend to be over-full of care for children, relatives, friends, always finding something that should be put right. They are continually correcting what they consider wrong, and enjoy doing so. They desire that those for whom they care should be near them.

Vervain (31)
Those with fixed principles and ideas, which they are confident are right, and which they very rarely change.

They have a great wish to convert all around them to their own views of life.

They are strong of will and have much courage when they are convinced of those things that they wish to teach.

In illness they struggle on long after many would have given up their duties.

Vine (32)
Very capable people, certain of their own ability, confident of success.

Being so assured, they think that it would be for the benefit of others if they could be persuaded to do things as they themselves do, or as they are certain is right. Even in illness they will direct their attendants.

They may be of great value in emergency.

Beech (3)
For those who feel the need to see more good and beauty in all that surrounds them. And, although much appears to be wrong, to have the ability to see the good growing within. So as to be able to be more tolerant, lenient and understanding of the different way each individual and all things are working to their own final perfection.*

Rock Water (27)
Those who are very strict in their way of living; they deny themselves many of the joys and pleasures of life because they consider it might interfere with their work.

They are hard masters to themselves. They wish to be well and strong and active, and will do anything which they believe will keep them so. They hope to be examples which will appeal to others who may then follow their ideas and be better as a result.

Dr Bach's First Aid remedy

At the beginning of the 1930s Edward Bach discovered that a combination of five different essences was particularly effective as an emergency preparation – a rescue remedy.

This First Aid remedy contains in drop form:
Star of Bethlehem (29) for shock
Rock Rose (26) for fear and panic
Impatiens (18) for mental stress and states of tension
Cherry Plum (6) for despair
Clematis (9) for feelings of 'not being with it', often presaging fainting or unconsciousness.

Authors' note: The original words, somewhat cryptic in this particular instance, have led a good many commentators to suggest their own somewhat arbitrary interpretations here – as, for example, the recommendation of Beech as a remedy for intolerant, critical and judgemental attitudes. On the basis of our own experience we cannot support this. Where the states of mind listed under Beech are concerned, the point at issue is that such people have the well-being of their fellow human beings at heart, and are not just intolerant or critical. It should not be overlooked that Beech is listed under group seven – 'Over-care for welfare of others'!

The First Aid remedy *cream* additionally contains:

Crab Apple (10) for cleansing.

A story relates how Edward Bach used the First Aid remedy for the first time.

A small freighter, loaded to the gunwales with bricks and tiles, broke up off the coast at Cromer in a storm. The two sailors on board managed to clamber up the mast, which was still sticking up above the surf, where they hung on for hours until a lifeboat could reach them through the raging sea.

The younger of the two sailors was already unconscious and blue in the face when the rescuers got to him, his clothes stiff with sea-salt. Edward Bach moistened his lips with the rescue remedy to help him over the severe shock. The man immediately recovered consciousness, sat up and was able to be warmed and cared for.

Emergencies
The First Aid remedy is applied in all emergencies, be they major or minor, as for example in cases of
   deep worries
   bad news
   accident or misfortune
   minor cuts (by a knife, a blade, other instruments or tools, as well as wounds inflicted by pointed instruments such as needles)
   anxiety states
   shock, fear and panic
   deep despair
   overwhelming stress, and so on.
The First Aid remedy, however, is no substitute for qualified medical attention. Rather is it a form of First Aid, serving to calm the patient, to build up or restore his or her self-confidence and to promote rapid healing or recovery until a skilled practitioner can be found.

For this reason it is recommended that a small bottle of First Aid remedy be kept ready-prepared at home, in the car, at the workplace and/or in the handbag.

Use, dosage and practical tips

The most important indications for use are as follows:
1. With the healing flower essences it is the person, not the illness, that is treated (Harmony is the healer!).

What matters is not the name of the illness or symptom, but the patient's state of mind (fear, insecurity or whatever); the discordant resonances within the personality are brought back into tune with the harmonic vibrations of the soul or self.

2. Should political or economic factors ever make access to the healing flower essences impossible, we would draw attention to Edward Bach's own instructions for do-it-yourself preparation (see pages 25–6), as well as to Julian and Martine Barnard's outstanding book *The Healing Herbs of Edward Bach. An Illustrated Guide to the Flower Remedies* (see bibliography).

3. The easiest way of determining the correct remedy is to take the following series of alternative – or rather complementary – steps:

   (a) Find out which of the seven groups corresponds to the sufferer's current state of mind; then read the descriptions that go with the individual flower essences and take whichever one comes nearest to fitting the particular condition observed.

   (b) There are many people who prefer to be guided purely intuitively from within – that is, by the soul or self. In this case a pendulum, bio-tensor or similar device can be used.

The flower colour cards   For additional ease of reference in determining the correct healing flower essences and their respective vibrations, we have developed the first flower colour cards, which we shall be introducing and explaining separately (see pages 127–30).

It may well be that more than one remedy seems to fit. Experience suggests that combinations of remedies are perfectly in order; many experts recommend a maximum of three, others as many as six. For preference, start with a maximum of three.

It is our experience that ingenious, complicated approaches, far from helping, actually tend rather to confuse the issue. Edward Bach, in the only book he ever wrote about the healing flower essences and their use, made the point quite clearly: 'No science, no knowledge is necessary, apart from the simple methods described herein.'

Preliminary remarks on dosage   Since the healing flower essences are pure and harmless, one need have no fear of taking too much of them, or too often, even though only a few drops are needed for effective treatment. None of the remedies can do any harm – as in the event, for example, of choosing the wrong remedy.

A reminder, meanwhile: if it is the right *vibration* that heals, then it is not the quantity, but the quality of the remedy that counts.

Dosage The healing flower essences are normally supplied in small 'stock bottles' containing the essences in the form of concentrates.

Take 2 (two!) drops of the appropriate concentrate and put them into a medium-sized medicine bottle or a 20 or 30cc dropper bottle.

Now fill this latter with pure, fresh well or spring water; in the event of uncertainty about the purity of the water, or if cold tap water is used, add a teaspoonful of brandy to 'preserve' the water. Distilled water is not recommended, as it is 'dead'. (Both the stock bottles and the solution itself should be stored in a cool place, especially in warmer climes.)

Thus, you now have a bottle containing just 2 to 4 drops of the healing flower essence – or possibly 2 times 2, or 3 times 2, if two or three different healing flower essences have been selected as suitable and mixed in together.

(**Important**: The First Aid remedy counts as *one* remedy only, even though it consists of five different essences.) From this bottle

- take 4 drops 4 times a day as a rule, directly on the tongue or dissolved in a little water or fruit juice, retaining it in the mouth for a while before swallowing. Note that
- the most benefit is gained if the healing flower drops are taken first thing in the morning and last thing at night, and that
- the length of treatment depends on how long the disharmonious state of mind lasts – and not on how long the disease symptoms persist.

Edward Bach further recommended

- that in emergency a few drops be taken every few minutes until some change occurs,
- in severe cases every half-hour or so
- and in chronic cases every 3 or 4 hours as the patient desires;

- that in the case of unconsciousness the lips should be moistened;
- that damp compresses may be applied in the case of pains, inflammation or similar conditions, with a few drops from the stock bottle being poured into a basin of water and this water then being used to moisten the compress;
- that in the meantime it may also prove helpful to pour a few drops of the appropriate remedy into the bathwater or on to the sponge.

First Aid remedy cream

The First Aid remedy cream is used externally, just as *all* the healing flower-drops can equally be used externally.

The cream may be spread thinly on bites, burns, strains, sprains, sores and so on.

The drops (from the solution or, in emergency, directly from the stock bottles themselves) can be trickled on to a damp cloth or sponge in order to moisten the forehead, cheeks, temples or other affected parts of the limbs or body.

Both the cream and the diluted drops can be used for massage.

As an emergency treatment, the First Aid remedy drops are often applied directly in undiluted form to the tongue, forehead or other affected parts of the body (but not to open wounds!).

The healing flower essences produce no side-effects of any kind. There is no danger from wrong dosage or over-dosage. They do not interact adversely with other prescribed medicines, nor is their own efficacy affected by them.

Sources and availability

Subject to legal regulations, healing flower essences are also obtainable from all good chemists (as we go to print, many natural remedies are under threat of banishment from the free market in deference to the interests of certain pharmaceutical concerns, materialistically-minded 'health experts' and health ministries, as well as sundry politicians who think they know best what is good for us). If desired, experienced chemists will prepare the chosen solutions according to the customer's specification, or on prescription.

It is a matter for debate whether it was ever wise to announce or list the healing flower essences as 'medicines' in West Germany in the first place, or whether those involved might not have been better advised to market them as 'foodstuffs', thus freeing them from all medical sales-restrictions. In the USA and the UK, for example, the healing flower remedies can be obtained without difficulty in alternative and health-food shops.

Should it ever become the case – as hopefully it will never do – that the essences cease to be freely available at all, a brief guide to do-it-yourself preparation will, as indicated earlier, be found on pages 25–6. In the following chapters, too, we shall be explaining in detailed, practical terms how to combine other natural healing methods effectively with the healing flower essences in such a way as to complement and reinforce them.

First, though, here is a handy reference table to the healing flower essences:

The healing flower essences in summary

Healing flower reference list
arranged according to Dr Bach's seven major groups

	1. Fear	Page
Rock Rose (26)	*Helianthemum nummularium*	11
Mimulus (20)	*Mimulus guttatus*	11
Cherry Plum (6)	*Prunus cerasifera*	11
Aspen (2)	*Populus tremula*	11
Red Chestnut (25)	*Aesculus carnea*	11
	2. Uncertainty	
Cerato (5)	*Ceratostigma willmottiana*	12
Scleranthus (28)	*Scleranthus annuus*	12
Gentian (12)	*Gentiana amarella*	12
Gorse (13)	*Ulex europaeus*	12
Hornbeam (17)	*Carpinus betulus*	12
Wild Oat (36)	*Bromus ramosus*	12
	3. Not sufficient interest in present circumstances	
Clematis (9)	*Clematis vitalba*	13
Honeysuckle (16)	*Lonicera caprifolium*	13
Wild Rose (37)	*Rosa canina*	13
Olive (23)	*Olea europaea*	13

3. Not sufficient interest in present circumstances (*Continued*)

White Chestnut (35)	*Aesculus hippocastanum*	13
Mustard (21)	*Sinapis arvensis*	13
Chestnut Bud (7)	*Aesculus hippocastanum*	14

4. Loneliness

Water Violet (34)	*Hottonia palustris*	14
Impatiens (18)	*Impatiens glandulifera*	14
Heather (14)	*Calluna vulgaris*	14

5. Over-sensitive to influences and ideas

Agrimony (1)	*Agrimonia eupatoria*	15
Centaury (4)	*Centaurium erythraea*	15
Walnut (33)	*Juglans regia*	15
Holly (15)	*Ilex aquifolium*	15

6. Despondency or despair

Larch (19)	*Larix decidua*	15
Pine (24)	*Pinus sylvestris*	15
Elm (11)	*Ulmus procera*	16
Sweet Chestnut (30)	*Castanea sativa*	16
Star of Bethlehem (29)	*Ornithogalum umbellatum*	16
Willow (38)	*Salix vitellina*	16
Oak (22)	*Quercus robur*	16
Crab Apple (10)	*Malus sylvestris*	17

7. Over-care for welfare of others

Chicory (8)	*Cichorium intybus*	17
Vervain (31)	*Verbena officinalis*	17
Vine (32)	*Vitis vinifera*	17
Beech (3)	*Fagus sylvatica*	18
Rock Water (27)		18

The First Aid remedy does not belong to any of the seven groups, but stands quite independently.

Healing flower index
in alphabetical order, and according to the serial numbers
often used

A guide to do-it-yourself preparation

We should like to make it quite clear once again that do-it-yourself preparation is not recommended for normal purposes, but only for emergencies. (The difficulties involved in do-it-yourself preparation have to do – among other things – with the need for access to the absolutely fresh, healthy flowers of sturdy, naturally-growing plants, and these in such variety as is seldom to be found in a single locality.)

There are according to Edward Bach two methods of preparation: the 'sunshine method' and the 'boiling method'.

The sunshine method

Take a thin glass bowl and fill it with the purest water available (if possible from a nearby fresh, clean spring).

Pluck the relevant flowers from the plants and scatter them over the surface of the water so that the whole of it is covered with floating flowers.

Let the bowl of flowers stand for three or four hours in radiant sunlight (more briefly than this only if the flowers start to show the first signs of wilting).

Now take the flowers carefully out of the bowl and pour the water into clean bottles until they are half full.

Top up this water with approximately the same volume of brandy or cognac to preserve the aqueous medium.

What you now have is the familiar 'stock bottles' – but *not* the ready-to-use drops for direct application!

It is from these bottles that a few drops are now taken

in order to prepare the dosage bottles, as previously described (see page 21).

The solar method is used to prepare the following healing flower essences: Agrimony, Centaury, Cerato, Chicory, Clematis, Gentian, Gorse, Heather, Impatiens, Mimulus, Oak, Olive, Rock Rose, Scleranthus, Wild Oat, Vervain, Vine, Water Violet and White Chestnut flowers. Rock Water (healing water from natural springs that have not been 'domesticated' or 'engineered' in any way) can be preserved and used in the same way, once it has been left, freshly-drawn, to 'charge up' still further with sunshine in a glass bowl.

The boiling method The remainder of the healing flower essences are prepared by boiling them in clean, pure water for half an hour.

To finish, pour the liquid through a sieve or, better, through a clean linen cloth in a funnel, into bottles (not too cold, or they will crack), and let the mixture cool. Then top them up once again with brandy.

Further hints With Horse Chestnut Bud, pick the buds from the white chestnut tree just before they open.

With the other remedies, use not just the flowers for boiling, but small pieces of the stalk as well; if there are young leaves, add a few of these too.

Although many of these plants originally came from southern Europe and the Near East, they have since made themselves fully at home in central Europe and elsewhere.

Further information can be obtained from The Flower Remedy Programme, PO Box 65, Hereford HR2 0UW.

2. Colour-energy and health

The power of colour

As human beings we live in a world of colours. Nature positively abounds with colours. Colours are vibrational frequencies and thus energies. Colour is both light and life. And yet each individual colour is only a *part* of that light (it is a well-known fact that a prism will split up white sunlight into its constituent colours). Each colour is *part of a whole*. It is disharmony within this whole that leads to spiritual and physical dissonances within us, and ultimately to illness.

The conscious use of colours

This chapter is designed to offer practical help in using colours more consciously and in recognizing and applying their energies. How rarely, after all, do we take any conscious account of colours – or, to take actual examples, of the red of sunset and sunrise, the yellow of the sun, the blue of the sky, the white of fleecy, cotton-wool clouds or the black of thunder clouds, the green of the meadows, the varied colours of summer flowers, the yellow of autumn leaves, the white of the sand or the blue of the sea . . .

From literature we learn of romanticism's 'azure blooms'. Traditional wisdom has it that hope springs ever green, that love is like a red, red rose, that cowardice is yellow, loyalty true blue, mourning deepest black (though it is a matter of common knowledge that it is white among the Chinese) and purity shining white – whence, of course, the symbolism of the traditional pure white wedding gown and the proverbial 'gleaming white escutcheon'.

Indeed, the moment one starts to think about it, all kinds of other examples spring to mind. Merely to think about colours or to engage ourselves emotionally with them causes us to see inwardly, or even to feel, a whole rainbow-spectrum of hues. And in addition to the 'physical' colours there are certain people who are sensitive to an astonishing range of other, metaphysical or 'astral' colours, too.

Meanwhile, everyday speech does not limit itself to attaching colours to the world around us. We similarly characterize *ourselves* in terms of colours. 'He's got the blues,' we say. Somebody else is in a black mood. Yet another is yellow-hearted, green with envy, blue with cold, crimson with rage or excitement. And some people will lie until they are blue in the face.

Lovers see the world through rose-tinted glasses – as happens also to people who are over-enthusiastic about things and so are no longer capable of seeing reality *in its true colours*. Liars who are caught out are almost by definition left red in the face. We go white with shock or fear. We all know somebody who always looks on the dark side of things. We are keen, too, to check whether or not our friends come back from holiday with new colour in their cheeks.

Such colour-based terms did not arise by chance. They refer back to strictly concrete observations. People really do go crimson with anger or white as a sheet with shock.

When we say, 'You're green with envy' (or yellow, as the Germans prefer to put it), the person concerned is not normally (or at least, not yet) actually green or yellow in colour. And yet, if one is constantly consumed with envy, this can affect the liver, and eventually the gall bladder too. Failure in these areas can then actually lead to the skin or the whites of the eyes gradually taking on a yellowish or greenish tinge.

Psychospiritual causes: physical effects

This brings us to the connection between 'invisible' spiritual or mental causes and 'visible' physical effects. This, indeed, is the whole theme of this manual: how do our spiritual and mental 'vibes' influence our bodily well-being? What are the connections between body, mind and soul, or between perceptions, feelings, thoughts and our very being itself? How can we lead lives that are healthy, happy and whole?

People's colour preferences and their reactions to particular colours help the practitioner to draw certain conclusions about their attitudes to life, their state of mind and even their physical condition. An example from our own practice will illustrate this.

A young lady of our acquaintance has a generalized aversion to red. She first became directly aware of this one day when she went into a room the south-facing window of which was covered by a red curtain through which sunlight was streaming. She became physically sick, felt all kinds of aggressive impulses arising within her and had to leave the room.

This woman is constitutionally predisposed to be (as we say) of a sanguine temperament. She is more easily excited than, for example, a phlegmatic or melancholy type. But in such cases there are also other causes to be researched, such as 'uncertainty' and/or 'loneliness' under the terms of the healing flower groups, or fear of confronting the active forces of 'nature red in tooth and claw', if we are to investigate the case in terms of depth-psychology.

It is at this point that holistic forms of diagnosis (involving constitutional typology, Kirlian photography, facial diagnosis and plain intuition) and various therapies (healing flower essences and colour therapy, for example, using complementary colours and the like) duly comes into play. They contribute tangibly to improving the patient's physical condition by promoting harmony on the psychic level.

We have already said that colour is life. Life is a creative development that unfolds according to particular laws and cycles. In the colours, meanwhile, particular laws and cycles of life are similarly reflected. We human beings have been investigating both life and light for thousands of years, yet still there are no incontestable conclusions or unanimous findings. For the free operation of mind and spirit allows and demands nothing short of variety and multiplicity.

It is our intention in the next section to offer an admittedly somewhat subjective summary of the whole system of colours and their meaning. This summary is intended as a framework to help each individual discover and develop his or her own relationships to the various colours. It should thus provide an aid not only to 'getting to know colour', but also to living consciously with it.

The cardinal numbers one to nine are a key to this summary.

One

In the beginning is the *primal light*, which encompasses the spiritual totality, or wholeness, of all the colours. This primal light is creation's point of departure. In conjunction with the primal sound, it brings about the transition from formlessness to form. It is transparent, and so can also be described as 'light without colour'.

Two

From the primal light follow the light and darkness of the material planes – namely *white* and *black*. These are not colours in the normal sense, but rather polarities or opposites. (Complementary colours such as red and green, for example, are in no way opposite to each other, but merely mutually fulfilling.)

This polarity finds its expression in the Yin-Yang symbol of the orient – interestingly enough, often not merely in black and white, but also in silver and gold. Yin and Yang are also seen as feminine and masculine respectively (not, though, as 'good' and 'bad'!).

In our material world every light must cast a shadow. Where there is light, consequently, there is also shadow.

On the basis of their vibrational energies, our familiar earthly colours can be divided into Yin and Yang, positive and negative, feminine and masculine, bright and dark – though some of them are also neutral in their effects.

Three

Only through the splitting of white light do *the three primary colours blue, red and green* arise. They can also be called *pure* colours, by contrast with the mixed secondary colours.

When blue, red and green light are mixed together, they produce white!

It is on the three primary light colours of blue, red and green (see illustration) that many (though not all) colour theories are based (see also the details given under the number 'Six').

Blue is primarily Yin, negative, feminine, passive and cool:

Red is primarily Yang, positive, masculine, active and warm:

Green is primarily neutral.

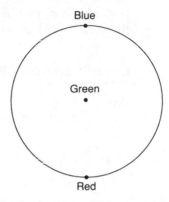

Light's *secondary colours* (or mixtures) are *yellow, blue-green* and *magenta.*

The customary way in which the pigments used in painting are distinguished is quite different, however. Here it is red, blue and yellow that are said to be the primary colours, while orange, violet and green are said to be complementary colours.

If we now consider the familiar trinity of body, soul and spirit within the framework of the pigments, then

Red, being the densest colour, corresponds to the body and its powers;

Yellow, being the brightest, corresponds to the spirit (in this case the mind and consciousness); and

Blue, as the most restrained, corresponds to the soul.

It is apparent, then, that everything depends on the particular standpoint from which one undertakes to divide up the colours. No single standpoint or its consequent assignment of colours necessarily contradicts another, let alone excludes it. Indeed, it is perfectly right and proper that there should be a variety of ways of approaching the topic, all capable of supplementing each other.

Four

In his by now world-famous *Lüscher test*, the Swiss psychologist Max Lüscher uses four colours as a tool for psychological assessment. To the three primary pigments he adds the colour green.

As he sees it, red stands for self-confidence, blue for contentment, yellow for freedom and green for self-respect. He describes how the ability of 'four-colour people' to live life to the full consists in the right application of these four skills or inner feelings, and sets out these relationships as follows:

Colour	Impression	Behaviour	Inner feeling
Red	brings excitement	and activity	thus, self-confidence (feeling of personal power)
Blue	brings peace	and satisfaction	thus, contentment (integration)
Green	brings firmness	and perseverance	thus, self-respect (identity)
Yellow	brings release	and change	thus, freedom (self-development)

(From Max Lüscher, *Der 4-Farben-Mensch*.)

Five
The *five elements* of ancient wisdom correspond to *five colours*:

Water = adaptation = blue
Earth = perseverance = green
Fire = power = red
Air = give-and-take = yellow
Ether = spirit = violet (or iridescence – rather like mother-of-pearl, which shimmers with all the colours at once)

The Indian *Sant Mat Yoga* and other age-old doctrines are based on the following theory of elements:
- In plants one element is active, namely water.
- In reptiles two elements are active, namely water and earth.
- In birds there are three, namely water, earth and air.
- In mammals there are four, namely water, earth, air and fire.
- In humans there are five, namely water, earth, air, fire and ether.

This is also the source of one of the basic insights that inform vegetarianism: one eats plants because only one element is active (that is, conscious) within them, and interference in the natural order is thus kept to an absolute minimum.

Six

In the *colour-circle* as devised by Goethe and applied by the many followers of his teachings we find six colours – the three primary colours blue, red and yellow, and the associated mixtures violet, orange and green.

Orange and yellow are said to be Yang, positive, bright, warm and active;

Violet and blue are said to be Yin, negative, dark, cool and passive;

Red can be either, according to its particular shading (according to Goethe's theory of colour, purple counts as the strongest colour-pole and the centre of the whole colour-system);

Green is said to be the neutral, reconciling, soothing mid-point of all the colours.

The colour-circle gives a good idea of the relationships between the colours, their complementary colours, their allocation to Yin and Yang and so on. At the same time, though, it represents only one possible approach to the subject.

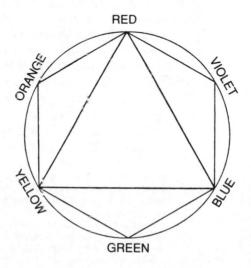

Seven

The *seven chakras* or main human energy centres are, like the elements, characterized by colours.

Allocation of chakras, functions and colours

Name	Function	Colour
7 Crown centre	Access to creativity	Violet
6 Brow centre	Seat of the soul or self	Deep blue
5 Throat centre	Power of inspiration	Turquoise
4 Heart centre	Transpersonal love	Yellow*/Pink
3 Abdominal centre	Seat of the ego or 'I'	Green*
2 Sexual centre	Power of reproduction	Orange*
1 Base centre	Primal life-force	Red*

The spleen is the organ for taking up sunlight. Many authors either combine the spleen and its subsidiary chakra with the main chakra of the solar plexus, or attempt to replace this latter entirely with the spleen centre. Perhaps that is why the abdominal centre is associated with yellow. (In the practical section you will find that colour therapy is based on vibrational states and symptoms, not on intellectually laid down systems of assignment. According to Dr Jay Scherer, pink qualifies as a 'heart' colour.)

There are various names for the chakras or energy centres. Thus, the crown chakra is also called the *sahasrara*, while the abdominal centre is also called the naval centre or the solar plexus centre. (This is not to be confused with the energy centre for physical strength and psychological calm that lies just below the navel, and that we know from the Japanese and Chinese as the 'centre of the world' or as *hara*.)

One particular error that is often to be found in publications by Western writers concerns the sexual and base

Opinions are divided here: in the Orient the heart centre is sometimes portrayed as yellow or gold and the abdominal centre as green, whereas modern Western authors overwhelmingly give green for the heart centre and yellow for the abdominal centre. True, there are associations here with the sequence of colours in the rainbow, which thus tends to favour the oriental view. On this basis green, as the balancing, neutral colour in the middle of the spectrum corresponds to the human would-be target state in the midst of the body (the belly) and to the ego. Yellow, gold and pink are aspects of transpersonal love translated into colour terms, and so are generally assigned to the region of the heart.

centres. Quite often both are treated as a single chakra, thus confusing the reproductive power of the sex organs with the primal life-force and sheer survival drive of the base centre. Here as elsewhere, personal observation and experience are the best tools for arriving at a valid personal judgement.

Eight

The colour researcher and healer Theo Gimbel refers to *eight colours* of the spectrum. The first seven are (1) red, (2) orange, (3) yellow, (4) green, (5) turquoise, (6) blue and (7) violet. The *eighth* colour is magenta. This is the way things turn out if one no longer thinks of the spectrum in linear form, as sketched out above, but as a closed circle. It is then that the new colour magenta – a deep red-violet – appears between red at the lower and of the familiar rainbow spectrum and violet at its upper end.

Gimbel sets out his allocation of these eight colours to the various energy centres, functions and glands as follows

8	High spirituality, individuality	Magenta
7	Pineal gland, crown	Violet
6	Pituitary gland, 'third eye'	Blue
5	Thyroid gland, throat	Turquoise
4	Cardinal plexus, heart	Green
3	Solar plexus, abdomen	Yellow
2	Suprarenal glands	Orange
1	Sacral plexus, base	Red

(After Gimbel, *Healing through Colour*, p. 63, see bibliography.)

Gimbel's allocation cf the suprarenal glands to the second chakra, and the sacral plexus and gonads to the first chakra, finds no general support. The more usual arrangement allocates the sacral plexus and gonads – that is, the sexual centre – to the second chakra, and the suprarenal glands – the organic equivalent of the base centre – to the first chakra.

Gimbel, though, does make two interesting suggestions on the subject of light:

1. He describes *darkness* as *autonomous energy* which, although it cannot be measured (how, after all, can one possibly measure nothing?), nevertheless has its place not only in the creation of the

world but also in the development of consciousness
and in colour therapy.

2. He also asserts that colour has a *higher vibration*
than sound, and that in consequence colours are
more effective therapeutically than sounds, by analogy with the homoeopathic principle that higher
(that is, more dilute) potencies have higher vibrations and thus greater effectiveness than remedies
with lower frequencies.

Here, meanwhile, is another possible arrangement of the
colours and energy centres:

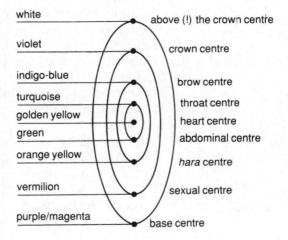

white	above (!) the crown centre
violet	crown centre
indigo-blue	brow centre
turquoise	throat centre
golden yellow	heart centre
green	abdominal centre
orange yellow	*hara* centre
vermilion	sexual centre
purple/magenta	base centre

Nine

With the number nine we come to the last in our number
sequence. This number refers to the end of a cycle, process or development. For this reason we propose at this
point to indicate the *nine inner colours* that can be experienced in dreams, visions or meditations.

The Indian philosopher and yoga master Sri Aurobindo
describes the meaning of the nine colours that appear to
the inner eye as follows:

Golden light: The light of truth, the light of the
higher spirit (modified according to one's stage of
development).

White light: The light of the power of pure consciousness,
from which all else arises.

Yellow: The light of the human spirit, before it encoun-
ters the golden light of divine truth.

Red: The colour of the physical: when touched by the higher light it turns into golden red. (Deep red light entering the physical realm has the effect of modifying this.)

Blue: The fundamental colour of divine bliss. (The many shades of blue are difficult to define, but the deeper shades tend to indicate the higher spirit, the paler shades the enlightened spirit.)

Green: Life, the rich outpouring of life energies: often, too, the power of living emotion.

Violet: The light of divine pity and mercy.

Purple: The colour of the life-force.

Diamantine light: This breaks forth from the heart of divine consciousness and brings about self-opening to divine consciousness.

(The colours of psychic light correspond to whatever they manifest. Psychological love, for example, is pink or rose, psychological purity white and so on.)

(translated from the German version of Sri Aurobindo's *Synthesis of Yoga*, see bibliography.)

And so we reach the end of this summary. Possibly you will feel somewhat overwhelmed by the mass of different indications and interpretations. The more you use this book as a practical guide, however, the more likely you are to find the information useful. The next step is deliberately to apply colour and light to the restoration of bodily and spiritual harmony – that is, of holistic health.

Simple self-help using colour therapy

Colour and mood

More or less conscious self-help through colour therapy starts first thing in the morning. According to your mood and purpose you reach for a blue or yellow blouse or shirt, a pair of grey or green trousers, a red tie or white neck-scarf. And what colours does your bathroom radiate? Do you feel at ease in it? Does it give you a positive attitude to the new day first thing in the morning?

This section offers a brief introduction on how to handle light and colour properly. We can distinguish between two ways of dealing with light and colour:

1. their more or less conscious application in *everyday life*, and

2. *specific colour therapy* as a method of psychosomatic treatment.

'Everyday use' covers, among other things:
  clothing
  hair colour and tinting
  cosmetic colourings (lips, cheeks, eyes, fingernails)
  jewellery (the colours of metals, stones etc.)
  house decoration (walls, wallpaper, curtains, floors,
    carpets, upholstery, tablecloths etc.)
  lighting (at home, at the workplace, in the restaurant)
  colour of car (exterior and interior)
  flower decorations, garden plants
  food and drink

No doubt you will be able to find further examples from daily life in which light and colour play a role. Because, though, the subject of this book is *healing through the 'right vibrations'*, we shall be offering no general interpretations or advice on everyday life at this point (such matters will have to await a further book). What you will find on the following pages are concrete therapeutic procedures (which may nevertheless have important implications for everyday usage). In no way, however, do these render superfluous either responsible decision-taking or the consultation of trained practitioners.

Nevertheless, what we shall have to say about the effects of the respective colour-vibrations in the context of specific psychosomatic therapies may still be transferred by a process of analogy to the use of light and colour in everyday life.

Healing through colour
Colour therapy may be counted among the most effective of healing techniques. It is painless and worry-free. Colour in the form of visible light frequencies is an ideal way of balancing discordant vibrations which ultimately are always the cause of illness. Colour, after all, exercises a bridging function between directly perceptible physical and emotional states and the invisible (though no less real) psychospiritual realm.

Moreover, rapid harmonization of the vibrations concerned, whether following colour therapy or after the taking of healing flower essences or other natural remedies (homoeopathy, tissue-salts and so on) can be directly and visibly demonstrated by Kirlian photography (see Chapter 5).

The seven major therapeutic colours

There now follows a description of the characteristics of the seven major therapeutic colours and a summary of the various forms of therapy involved. You may refer to them on the pages listed:

There are two pairs of complementary colours – in the first place orange and blue, and in the second yellow and violet. Turquoise occupies a special position that we shall be discussing at the end.

Red **Meaning**

Red is the warmest, most powerful and most enlivening of the colours.

Red signifies (physical) life.

Red is the colour of the blood.

Red, as the central life-energy, can be either masculine, Yang and active, or feminine, Yin and passive (see the colour-circle on page 56).

Red is vigour and heat, but by the same token the violence and destructiveness of fire, too.

Red signifies all that is inflammatory.

Red stands symbolically for conflict, passion and aggression.

Red is said to be the colour both of the heart and of love (more so, at any rate, than that particularly refined form of red which is pink).

In view of the fact that red spans the whole spectrum from the essential life-force and heartfelt love on the one hand to passionate energy extending to actual aggression and destructiveness on the other, red must be handled carefully in the context of colour therapy (see the warning given right at the end of this section).

Red is applied in colour therapy wherever the life-force needs to be stimulated or renewed, or where blocked life-energies need to be encouraged to flow harmoniously again.

Therapy
Red

- can release *chronic* obstructions and block-ages;
- can revivify organic functions that have degenerated;
- can stimulate the metabolism and promote elimination;
- can counter sluggish digestion and have a helpful, purgative effect;
- can further encourage creativity in those who already feel well.

Practical examples
In the case of a chronically blocked up nose, both sides of the nose (see points in the top illustration) may be irradiated with red light in order that the patient may breathe freely again.

The same goes for any loss of sense of smell arising from chronic obstruction of the nose.

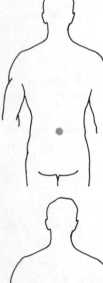

A case drawn from our practice will illustrate the point. A thirty-year-old female patient had been unable to breathe through her nose or to smell anything for two years. Five minutes of irradiation with red and a few drops of various healing flower remedies were sufficient to free her nose for breathing once again and restore her sense of smell. This first treatment was effective for three days. Two further treatments within a month were necessary to bring about long-term healing.

Again, if the onset of menstrual bleeding is particularly difficult, irradiation with red at the bottom of the lumbar vertebrae may be indicated (see middle illustration).

In addition, red has the effect of compensating for any lack of libido (that is, sexual potency, not desire!) either in women or in men. To this end red light is applied to the back of the pelvis at the level of the sex centre (see middle illustration).

In the case of sluggishness of the kidneys resulting from too little fluid intake and leading to pains in the back, irradiation of the area to the left and right of the lumbar vertebrae can have a healing effect (for the information of practitioners, on the bladder meridian). See the bottom illustration.

Another example from our practice will illustrate the point. A forty-year-old manager whose only fluid intake was coffee and occasionally wine came to us complaining of severe, generalized backache in the lumbar region. A visit to the orthopaedic specialist brought no improvement. My initial diagnosis, derived from routine Kirlian photography, revealed that the patient had been taking far too little in the way of pure liquids and that the kidneys had consequently become obstructed, so leading to the backache already referred to. The therapy took the form of an irradiation with red at the end of each kidney, administration of the appropriate healing flower essences and a complete change of regime involving a daily fluid intake of two to two-and-a-half litres of pure liquid (water or herb tea, but certainly no coffee).

An eight-year-old girl, similarly, was constantly waking up in the morning with swollen eyelids, feeling tired and listless and complaining of headaches in the neck region. When she visited our practice, facial diagnosis and Kirlian photography backed up by simple interrogation revealed that she was taking next to no fluids at all. The most that she was drinking was a cup of cocoa in the morning and a glass of thick, sweet fruit juice in the evening. What turned out to be helpful in this case was irradiation with red light in the middle of the ball of the foot (see illustration) together with further healing flower essences from the 'Uncertainty' group and a change of drinking habits to harmonize the kidney function and restore its flow.

In the case of sluggishness of the metabolism – constipation or sluggish bowels, for example, or skin impurities – irradiation with red on the so-called 'large intestine either of points' on the hands is recommended (see illustration).

These have merely been a few applications selected from among a wide range of possibilities. Feel free to apply red accordingly, then, on the basis of the guidelines laid down above.

Bear in mind, though, that it is often only the right *combination* of natural remedies such as colour therapy, healing flower essences and tissue-salts that turn out to have any lasting effect.

Please also bear in mind that, while any natural therapy can be an enormous aid to healing, many conditions will already have reached the stage where they are irreversible by the time treatment is sought (thus, severe kidney failure

– as, for example, in the case of a patient on dialysis – cannot be healed by colour therapy).

Warning! Too much red, too prolonged an exposure, application to unsuitable parts of the body or to inflamed areas, and/or use with patients who have an over-active thyroid or a choleric, aggressive temperament can easily lead to over-stimulation of the bodily functions through over-excitement of the nervous system. Actual aggression – be it open or repressed – can then result.

An anecdote will emphasize the point.

A painter was given the job of painting a small room red. He found instinctively that he had to leave the room every five or ten minutes to take a few deep breaths, let his breathing settle down again and allow his increasing feelings of nausea to subside. At the end of the job he asked the person employing him why the room had to be painted red. The other answered, 'I am a boxer. If I train for ten or fifteen minutes in a red room before every fight, I always win.'

If red vibrations are predominant in the body and produce a corresponding disharmony, what is needed is the complementary colour. This leads us from the two-edged colour that is red to the neutral, healing colour that is green.

Green   **Meaning**

Green is the most settling and calming of the colours.

Green signifies (physical) growth.

Green, in the form of chlorophyll, lies at the very basis of the process that supplies the oxygen we breathe.

Green stands for nature's ability to give structure and substance.

Green goes with biliousness.

Green nevertheless also symbolizes hope.

Green brings contentment and healing.

As a neutral healing colour, green is quite harmless to handle. The healing colour *par excellence*, it is used in colour therapy principally in order to soothe irritations, smooth out discordant vibrations and give substance to new life structures.

Therapy
Green

- can cure *acute* obstructions and blockages;
- can soothe and heal feverish, inflammatory, swollen, painful and generally 'red' disease processes;
- has a beneficial effect on 'visual purple', and can thus ease eyestrain and even reduce any visual disturbances (combined, in cases of short-sightedness, for example, with the Bates method);
- can even-out mood swings and bring a new equanimity into states of discontentment and impatience.
- can boost feelings of self-worth in those who are insecure.

Practical examples

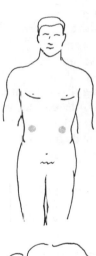

In cases of acute and painful gall bladder obstruction, irradiation with green light can restore the flow of bile.

A case in point from our own practice was a boy of about ten who came to me with his mother. Since the morning in question he had had undefined stomach-ache and had been suffering from frontal headache and extreme nausea. It then came out in conversation that he had attended a carnival the day before, where he had eaten doughnuts soaked in fat, as well as chips. Irradiation with green on the costal arch and the eyebrows (see illustrations), the First Aid remedy, and Nat. Sulph. and Kali Sulph. from the Schüssler tissue-salts (see Chapter 4) led to an immediate easing of the headache as well as to the subsequent disappearance of the other conditions. (Such gall blockages can be avoided by giving up animal fats more or less completely, and especially by not eating them hot or in fried dishes.) Kirlian photography before and afterwards confirmed the respective findings.

Green is indicated for all inflammations, as, for example, in the case of ear inflammations and toothache.

We are keen to take this opportunity once again to point out that colour therapy is of course no replacement for treatment by a qualified practitioner. What we are concerned with here is the adoption of a holistic approach to healing designed to promote health on *all* levels – not merely physical and material, but also psychological, emotional and spiritual.

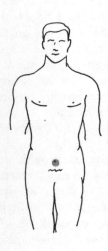

A little while ago my six-year-old son Daniel awoke in the night with violent toothache. I let him do the irradiation of the affected tooth from the outside of the cheek himself. This treatment was repeated twice more that same night. The toothache disappeared, never to return. To back up this treatment, I had him press with the thumbnail of his free hand on the 'toothache point' of his index finger (see top illustration). A visit to the dentist proved unnecessary in this case, as the cause of the pain was simply the eruption of a new molar.

For inflammations, the rule of thumb is to shine green light directly on the painful spot or wound. Green encourages regeneration and the formation of new cells. It is recommended after dental work or extractions, for earaches, bruises and bleeding.

If the nose is not blocked (see 'Red'), but constantly runs, then a degree of inflammation is already present. This is a cue to irradiate the left and right sides of the nostrils with green (see second illustration).

Many people, especially women, suffer alternately from constipation and diarrhoea, mainly as a result of the misuse of laxatives that are in any case unsuitable. In nearly every case there is an inflammation of the mucous lining of the gut. For reducing and healing this inflammation, and as a supplement to other kinds of therapy (change of diet, healing flower essences, homoeopathy, tissue-salts), green should be shone on the 'large intestine point' between thumb and index finger and around the navel (see bottom two illustrations).

For harmonizing states of impatience, discontent and insecurity, irradiation with green on the Yang aspect of the body – that is, on the back, just above the waist – can prove successful (see illustration opposite).

The beneficial influence of green, and particularly the living green of nature, is well known. People, especially those who wear glasses, who often sit for long hours in front of a computer or television screen, or who have a lot of written work to do, should make frequent breaks to relax both eyes and nerves. In the last resort, if no view of the natural world (without glasses!) is available, it helps to allow the eyes to come to rest on green houseplants, or on green curtains, pictures and so on.

Orange **Meaning**

Orange is the most active and energetic of the colours.

Orange signifies expansion, extroversion and outwardly-orientated living.

Orange has, of all colours, the greatest visual impact (which is why road-workers wear orange protective clothing and children carry similarly coloured satchels).

Orange stands for warmth, cheerfulness and openness.

Orange has the greatest healing effect on melancholy and depression.

Since orange is a mixture of red and yellow, similar precautions need to be taken as in the case of red. Thus, treatment should not be given too much or for too long to people of choleric temperament, in situations of conflict, in cases of inflammation or to the thyroid gland (see the one exception below, however).

Orange is applied in colour therapy above all when enjoyment of, and zest for, life have become lost or suppressed. As the active, Yang, complementary colour to blue's passive Yin, orange helps to return patients from exaggerated spirituality and reclusiveness to healthy physicality.

Therapy

Orange

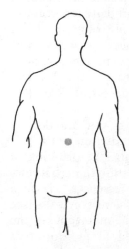

- can stimulate the digestion;
- can release stomach cramps attributable to the pressure of stored-up problems;
- can support the spleen and reduce somewhat the effects of environmental toxins and the side-effects of vaccinations;
- can inject enjoyment into living and transform despair, depression, melancholy and heavy-heartedness into a new zest for life;
- can have a generally problem-solving, opening and activating effect.

Practical examples

Orange helps with sluggish digestion, with obstructions of the spleen as a result of environmental toxins (noticeable in children mainly in the form of 'stitch' in the side), with vaccinations and stomach-aches – both in the form

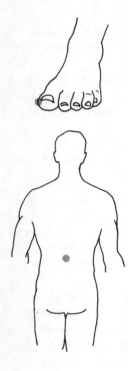

of stomach-cramps associated with personal problems and of more generalized stomach-aches in children.

A fourteen-year-old boy came to our surgery with his mother. He was complaining of stomach-ache and the 'stitch'. Kirlian diagnosis revealed obstructions of the spleen and severe psychological problems. In conversation it emerged that the youngster felt rejected by his schoolmates and for this reason no longer wanted to participate in lessons. He was given healing flower essences from the 'despondency and despair' group and an irradiation with orange light on the big toes and in the middle of the back (see illustrations).

The stomach-ache disappeared even while the irradiation was being given. Inside a week he recovered his zest for life: he started enjoying lessons more and wanted to play with his schoolfriends again.

As we pointed out above, orange is the most effective colour for countering depressions and other, similar states of mind – as a further example from our practice will demonstrate.

A man of about thirty-five had long been in psychotherapy. He was suffering from severe depressions without any external cause. He had been prescribed tranquillizers and other mind-drugs. He came to our naturopathic practice because these remedies were bringing him no real healing and he was suffering the same wild mood swings as before. Besides which, he was keen to free himself from his dependency on daily medication.

The Kirlian photograph showed obstruction of the spleen (possibly caused by the medicines), a severely overstressed lymph system and – naturally enough – various anxiety states. Therapy turned out to be complex and protracted, but in the end proved successful. We shall merely sketch it out here.

The first step was to undertake 'drying-out' and detoxification therapy. This involved the irradiation of the gall bladder, liver, spleen and other points, the drinking of herb tea plus the additional administration of herbal tinctures, the taking of healing flower essences, classical homoeopathic remedies and the Schüssler tissue-salts (see Chapter 4), as well as 'cupping' and the massaging of the connective tissue. A dowser discovered, in addition, that the patient was sleeping with the head of his bed over an area of disturbing energy and so the bed was re-sited. The colour therapy was carried out twice weekly – above all in the form of irradiation with orange light on the big toes and various of the chakras. The mind-drugs were not withdrawn all at once, but reduced to nil gradually. Further natural remedies were given as required.

It was only after some six months, once the resulting detoxification and the natural remedies had taken effect, that the first improvement started to become apparent. After nine months or so the patient had recovered so much zest for life that he no longer suffered from depressions or needed the mind-drugs, and right up to this day has had no relapses to complain of. (The successful healing came about in this case partly as a result of the right therapy, but partly, too, because of the patient's will to recover and his confidence in the therapist.)

Some five years ago a woman in her late thirties turned up with generalized abdominal cramps. The gynaecologist had been unable to establish the presence of any organic disorder, and so the causes had to lie in the psychological or vegetative domain. The Kirlian photograph revealed that the problem had to do with an emotional blockage that was affecting the glands of the endocrine system. It emerged in conversation that the woman's quasi-marital relationship with the father of her child had broken up. She had had no further sexual relations with this man for a year ever since discovering that her partner was being unfaithful to her. Moreover she was not interested in any other man. For all this, she was a vivacious woman, attractive and full of life.

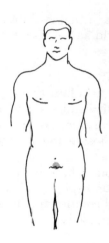

Apart from the First Aid remedy (for the shock of her discovery) and Star of Bethlehem (from the 'despondency and despair' group), it was above all colour treatment that caused the complete turnabout that followed. A single irradiation with orange at the upper edge of the pubic hair and a similar irradiation with the complementary colour blue on the site of the 'third eye' (see illustrations) caused the woman spontaneously to lose her abdominal pains, to regain her confidence and zest for life and to find herself able to turn to another man.

We shall conclude this section with a description of how to use the complementary colours orange and blue as a form of quick test.

Under normal circumstances, certain toxins (the so-called essential urinary components) are excreted in the urine. If, however, either the kidney function is disturbed and/or too little 'free' (that is, uncompounded) liquid is taken (in the form of water or herb tea, say), these toxins will often pass via the bloodstream into the head, where they can produce pressure in the head, headaches and even migraine attacks.

If, in cases of this type, irradiating the 'third eye' between the eyebrows with blue leads to pressure and tension, whereas irradiation of the same spot with orange brings about release and relaxation, the presence of such toxins in the head area is indicated. This test result then needs to be confirmed by Kirlian photography and classical forms of naturopathic diagnosis.

Blue　**Meaning**

Blue is the coolest, purest and deepest of the colours.

Blue corresponds to reserve, introversion and the inner life.

Blue stands for the unconscious, inner calm, gentleness and spiritual profundity.

Blue is also regarded as the colour of spiritual evolution, of longing for the non-material world and – in certain shades – of spiritual healing.

Blue symbolizes loyalty.

Blue is not a dangerous colour to use in colour therapy. One should merely avoid too long an irradiation with blue of people of a melancholy disposition, so as not to compound any tendency towards losing touch with reality.

Blue is important as a healing colour wherever functional disturbances of the pituitary (or hypophysis) are involved, and where both physical and emotional relaxation and clarity of consciousness are needed.

Therapy

Blue

- can lower the blood pressure;
- can cure organic complaints and cramps of nervous origin;
- serves as the most important healing colour for menopausal complaints;
- can help to cure nervous skin allergies;
- can encourage suppurating wounds to heal;

- can ease the pain of circulatory blockages (for example, varicose veins and haemorrhoids);
- can promote relaxation and rest in cases of nervous insomnia;
- can have a quietening and purifying effect, as well as cooling tempers;
- can reduce swellings.

Practical examples

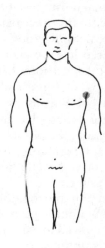

In cases of *temporary* high blood pressure, immediate irradiation with blue under the armpit is recommended (see illustration). In such cases, though, colour therapy is *not* suitable for effective long-term healing and *in no way* replaces expert treatment. Nevertheless it can ease such passing complaints as shortness of breath while climbing the stairs.

Irradiation with blue, in conjunction with the Schüssler tissue-salt Mag. Phos., can help with muscle cramps such as writer's cramp.

Blue can also ease stomach cramps *of nervous origin*, as well as nervous spasms of the eyelids or the Adam's apple, for example (the latter complaint being prominent among youngsters at puberty). In all such cases simply irradiate the site in question. (There is also nearly always a need for Mag. Phos. at the sixth decimal potency – see Chapter 4.)

The most common menopausal complaints are recognized as being hot flushes, mood swings and extreme over-sensitivity. However, the natural hormonal changes of the menopause do not *have* to be accompanied by these conditions. Healing flower essences (Walnut, for example), homoeopathy (depending on the particular symptom), and blue light can all help to speed up the transition and avoid the side-effects mentioned.

A woman of about fifty complained of hot flushes leading to the sudden blushing of her whole face, and also of uncontrollable outbreaks of sweating that merely compounded her mood swings since she found both symptoms particularly embarrassing. Her gynaecologist had prescribed hormonal treatment, but this had had side-effects, causing her to put on weight and suffer from digestive disturbances that merely added to her insecurity. In addition, she was grossly over-sensitive to comments and remarks from her family, who actually loved her very much. She took almost everything as a personal criticism. The woman came to naturopathy in order to try out some other kind of treatment. The therapy, which lasted three months, first of all treated her digestion and eventually left her totally free of all symptoms. Briefly, the main steps were as follows.

In addition to the complaints already described, Kirlian diagnosis revealed that the liver was being overworked by the effort to free the body of the additional hormones that were being administered. In tandem with any treatment of the menopausal problems, therefore, detoxification of the liver with the aid both of plant-based liver remedies and of irradiation with yellow light on the liver point had to be set in train. The hormone therapy was gradually reduced to zero. (The administration of hormones – which, after all, are not part of our natural diet – has the effect of partially putting out of commission the pituitary gland, which is normally responsible for regulating the body's hormones. This makes any natural self-regulation of the body more difficult, if not impossible.)

The actual therapy, though, consisted of homoeopathic remedies and healing flower essences (Walnut – plus, in this case, Centaury), both taken daily, as well as colour-treatment: blue to remove the 'heat' symptoms, orange to support the hormonal changes and yellow to stimu-late liver function. The irradiation was carried out twice weekly – blue on the nape of the neck, orange at the upper limit of the pubic hair and yellow on the liver points (see illustrations). I also recommended that she use more in the way of blue bedclothes and bedroom curtains, as well as making a point of wearing a blue scarf.

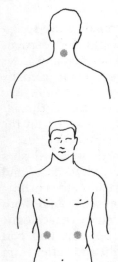

With particular allergies (sun-freckles, for example), suppurating wounds, varicose veins and haemorrhoids, blue is applied directly to the sites in question. The cool-ness of the blue will ease conditions of a 'feverish', nerve-based type, even if treatment on such occasions is not always restricted to blue only.

Blue is also useful for all kinds of burns.

Nervous disturbances such as sleeplessness, over-talkativeness and restlessness in children (the so-called 'fidgets') can be effectively reduced with the aid of blue.

Blue acquires a particular role in the context of colour treatment for addictions. All types of addiction, whether to alcohol, cigarettes, drugs (of whatever kind, including the supposedly harmless 'soft' ones), medicines and even money, power and so on can be traced back to disturbed functioning of the pituitary gland. The spiritual basis for all this is the loss of one's inner centre and of conscious relationship to the power of the soul. The 'seat of the soul' or self is said to be the 'third eye', which represents the subtle equivalent of the pituitary.

In addicts, that depth, fullness and colour, that richness and meaning that comes only from conscious experience of the soul as part of a greater creative order, are sought in substances and conditions that are of no more significance than mere passing passions. The more the spiritual energies are neglected or even denied, the more difficult it will be to find one's way out again without becoming embroiled in major breakdowns and fatal crises. For the effects of alcohol, tobacco, drugs and medicines can never be entirely removed, influencing as they do the finely-tuned system of so-called endocrine glands, including the pituitary's 'central control', both directly and indirectly.

We can go no further into detail here, except to say that any sensible addiction therapy will nevertheless start from the premises set out above. Thus, the aim of any holistic treatment must be to lead to the restoration of the conscious link with the soul or self. It is here that colour therapy can prove to be of sterling service, alongside the healing flower essences, homoeopathy, spiritual counselling and so on.

Blue tunes us more fully to the energy centre of the 'third eye' (see illustration) and helps to harmonize the pituitary gland. Blue helps to improve our knowledge of non-material truths and relationships.

In addition, *yellow* will, where necessary, promote rational understanding of why inner and outer transformation is needed in the first place.

Yellow **Meaning**
Yellow is a warm, cheerful, bright colour.
Yellow stands for a lively understanding, intellect and
    ability to analyse.
Yellow corresponds to openness and to a willingness to
    exchange views, as well as to flexibility and to interest
    in what is going on.

Yellow signifies intellectual drive, conceptual ability and sheer practicality, as well as ripeness for promotion.

Yellow symbolizes the solar frequency – that is, a state of mental stimulation – but also envy and jealousy.

Yellow is the colour of ripe corn, of 'golden October' and of maturity in general.

A particular point to note is that cholerics and people with over-active thyroids need to be circumspect in their use of yellow in colour therapy in order to avoid over-stimulation.

Yellow encourages the functioning of kidneys, liver and gall bladder as well of the lymph glands – that is, the production of bodily secretions. It stimulates the thought processes and interest in one's own life and environment, and consequently combats apathy.

Therapy
Yellow

- can raise the blood pressure;
- can reactivate a weakened stomach function, and help with kidney disturbances;
- can increase liver activity (as, for example, in jaundice) and thus give support to the liver's detoxification processes;
- can transform chronic functional disorders (of the lymph glands, for example) into acute conditions, and so improve the prospects of successful treatment;
- can promote a renewed interest in what is going on in those who are apathetic and listless;
- can awaken new hope in those who have become resigned to their fate (such as patients with long-term illnesses);
- can strengthen the life-force by way of the solar plexus.

Practical examples
Being a warm colour, yellow can raise the blood-pressure. It is interesting to note that the blood pressure responds less favourably to red (and, to some extent, to orange) than to the 'weaker' yellow. Low blood pressure can often be traced back to under-production of stomach juices.

Yellow stimulates the production of stomach juices (in such cases bitter herbs can also help). Yellow can be helpful wherever there is any disturbance in the production

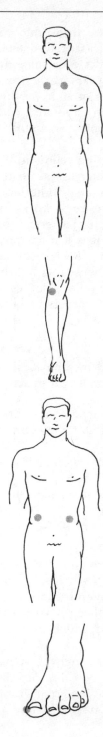

of bodily secretions – and thus for any kind of digestive deficiency – as well as where the body's detoxification processes are disturbed: in other words, it can help cure all kinds of functional weaknesses of the metabolism.

A thirty-six year old man came to our clinic complaining of gastric nausea and a feeling like a 'stone in the stomach', as well as of lack of appetite, plus exhaustion leading to fainting fits. After taking his blood pressure and carrying out Kirlian diagnosis, it soon became clear that his production of stomach juices was inadequate and his blood pressure too low.

Merely irradiating him with yellow on the fronts of the shoulders (see top illustration) at once rid him of the feeling of faintness and led to the spontaneous normalization of the blood pressure. In addition the stomach point just underneath the side of the knee (see second illustration) was irradiated with yellow four times during the next fortnight, while bitter herb remedies were taken daily and the healing flower remedy Honeysuckle was used to harmonize his attitude to life. After a fortnight's treatment he felt free of all symptoms.

On her first visit to our practice a young woman in her late twenties complained of slight general nausea, digestive irregularity, a tendency to swollen veins in the foot and intermittent slight headaches. The Kirlian photograph revealed inadequate liver function. At once the liver points at the edges of the rib-cage and on the big toes (see bottom two illustrations) were irradiated, and plant-based liver remedies prescribed. On the control photograph twenty minutes later, renewed activity of the liver was observable. The young woman felt visibly better and was free of symptoms for three or four weeks, though she had to give further support to the liver from time to time with plant-based liver remedies, and above all had to avoid alcohol (which she in any case could not tolerate).

In the context of the use of plant remedies for the liver, it is interesting to note that many 'liver plants' have yellow flowers, such as dandelion, celandine, marigold, St John's wort and cowslip or primrose.

If the kidneys and/or lymph glands need to be stimulated, yellow is applied to the corresponding points on the body. Diagnosis and treatment, though, should be left to the expert. Care should be taken when irradiating the lymph gland points if high blood pressure is present.

A further practical example comes from my co-author's own personal experience. Unpleasant, ill-defined feelings of 'blockage' in the lymph nodes ever since the extraction of a wisdom tooth two years earlier disappeared spontaneously inside a quarter of an hour after the exterior of his lower jaw had been irradiated with yellow for some three minutes. Treatment was still in progress at the time of writing.

There are no specific points for applying yellow in the context of colour therapy in order to increase academic enjoyment or keenness, whether in children or otherwise. Nor are there any for stimulating the desire to work, for increasing people's involvement in what is going on around them or for awakening their interest in shaping their own lives actively and consciously. Rather should the cheerful solar colour yellow be freely used within the personal environment – yellow flowers, yellow clothes, if necessary even yellow walls, yellow carpets, yellow folders in the office and so on.

Violet **Meaning**

Violet is the most strongly artistic and metaphysical of the colours, as well as being the colour of alchemy, magic and mysticism.

Violet has the highest vibrational frequency and at the same time the shortest wavelength of all the colours in the visible light spectrum.

Violet is regarded as the colour of cosmic energy, as also of radioactivity.

Violet stands for spiritual experience and consciousness (as well as the experience of suffering).

Violet is the colour of the New Age, or age of Aquarius, and is thus the colour of inspiration.

One has only to experiment with violet to establish that it normally has a pleasant, cooling effect. Nevertheless, prolonged irradiation of the crown centre with it can lead to headaches and melancholy, while at other points it can produce a certain 'prickly' tingling (in which case the balancing colour is yellow).

Violet is the colour that has the most strongly purifying effect on one's state of mind (especially on the spiritual level). With violet, any dissonances between polar vibrations such as Yin and Yang, active and passive, feminine and masculine can be ironed out.

Therapy
Violet

- can be applied either when external impurities are present or when the need for 'inner' purification is detected;
- can exercise a balancing effect on the vibrations of the two halves of the brain;
- can serve to open the consciousness to life experiences of a non-material type.

Practical examples and suggestions for use

A whole range of practical case histories can be adduced. Since violet operates as a healing colour mainly on the psychic level, though, its effects as experienced are even more subjective in character than with the other colours. For this reason the following are no more than suggestions for use, to which further systematic research needs to be applied.

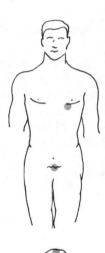

It has been shown that irradiation with violet (as with blue) causes wounds to heal more quickly. The use of the complementary colours violet and yellow in conjunction with the healing flower essence Crab Apple will be explained later.

One case worth mentioning from our own practice concerns a woman of very average gifts in her mid-fifties who was a singer, and whose loss of voice we were able to cure completely by irradiation with violet.

With acne, too, especially during puberty and where psychologically determined, violet has produced good results.

Violet is mainly applied to the front of the body on the heart centre, to the middle of the back, at the centre of the upper boundary of the pubic hair and to the crown centre on the top of the head (see illustrations).

Violet can stimulate the higher intuition, something which can be particularly important with highly intellectual and materially-orientated people (in this case too, in other words, it serves as the complementary colour to yellow). This involves balancing the vibrations of the two halves of the brain — the left-hand, active, masculine, extroverted, practical hemisphere and the right-hand, passive, feminine, introverted, artistic hemisphere. Bound up with this balancing process is often a harmonizing of the feminine and masculine powers, the *anima* and *animus*. At a time of new attitudes towards sex roles themselves, and the development of new forms of sensibility, consciousness and self-understanding that cannot help but go beyond mere sexuality, violet can open up to us vital psychological and metaphysical insights.

As a purifying colour, violet can also help in cases where one feels oneself affected by unfavourable influences or even 'entities'. As we hope to show in a further book, many people are especially receptive to such strong 'astral' influences when, unprotected by spiritual guidance from a spiritual master, for example, they are exposed by too vigorous an opening of the solar plexus (that is, too much yellow in the abdominal 'feeling centre') to feelings, thoughts and powers from 'beyond'.

Turquoise   For a number of reasons, turquoise occupies a special place in colour therapy.

In the first place, it has so far been used only very rarely. It does not appear in 'classical' colour-theory (compare Goethe's colour-circle) and for this reason has no agreed complementary role vis-à-vis any other colour. Even the familiar system of complementary colours, after all, is based purely on established conventions.

One possible arrangement might look like this:

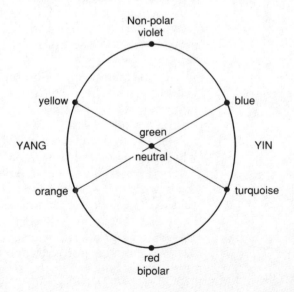

On the basis of oriental philosophical theories regarding the colours and chakras on the one hand, and of our experience of its practical application in the West on the other, we can now say, however, that turquoise is the colour of the throat centre. Greenish yellow seems a likely candidate for the role of complementary colour to it.

Meaning

Turquoise is a refreshing and cooling colour.

Turquoise goes with the power of creative thought, with clear linguistic expression and sincere communication.

Turquoise symbolizes truth.

Turquoise stands for the thyroid gland and its controlling functions, as well as the balancing out of unrecognized discordant emotions.

Turquoise is the vast vault of heaven above our earthly abode that allows us a glimpse of infinity.

Turquoise offers a bridge between the earthly and the ethereal.

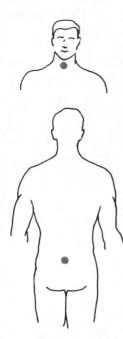

Therapy

Turquoise is used mainly to treat the thyroid gland when it has been stimulated into discordant activity, and also occasionally to harmonize the sex centre where a patient is over-sexed. It proves its worth, too, in cases of stress-based mental exhaustion, as also when the latter is caused by 'electromagnetic smog' (long working or leisure hours spent in front of unshielded computers or television sets, or in the neighbourhood of radio-transmitters, radar installations and so on).

Among the Pueblo Indians, window frames and door posts are traditionally painted turquoise to ward off evil spirits, turquoise having long been regarded as a sacred mineral by the Indians of Central America.

Turquoise is beamed onto the thyroid area and the sacrum, as shown on the illustrations.

White and black   Both white and black – that is, both light that contains all the colours and darkness that absorbs them all – have an important role to play in colour therapy.

Black

Black – that is, darkness, the absence of light or colour-stimulation of any kind – is needed principally when people are in a state of extreme exhaustion and/or suffering from psychosomatic over-excitement. The darkness first of all helps them to quieten down again. Colour treatment is then likely to be all the more effective. Hence, too, the importance of getting a good night's rest in natural darkness, so as to benefit from the thorough-going recuperation which sleep affords.

The long-term wearing of black is not to be recommended, as it either expresses concealed aggressive impulses and power drives or causes the wearer to absorb unfiltered energies from the world outside. (An example of such negative effects is the Nazi SS, with its cult of black magic.)

White

In the case of white, a distinction needs to be made between white light – which radiates the entire spectrum of colours combined into pure white – and white surfaces, which merely *reflect* white.

White is not used in *specific* colour therapy. Our current stage of earthly development is such that our individual illnesses are not as yet susceptible to healing by means of the external application of 'full-spectrum light'.

This does not mean, however, that we have to deny ourselves the vibrational energies of white light. On the contrary, the *non-specific* effects of white sunlight are actually vital for life, for without it we become ill – just as we do if we get too much of it! Too much white light 'burns us up', just as too much direct sunlight burns our skin.

For domestic or industrial lighting, so-called full-spectrum light is far from harmful. Lamps of this type are already available in the shops.

White in one's clothing and in interior decoration reflects light waves of every kind without filtering out any particular colour, but by comparison with sunlight or artificial light it has no radiant power of its own. Consequently it does not operate as a form of direct energy, but merely removes us from the influence of *particular* colours or other energies.

White in the clothing reflects a conscious orientation towards purity, clarity and freshness (if, that is, 'put on' airs of sanctity are not at the real basis of it).

The following key-phrases, then, will sum up what we have said about the use of colours in healing:

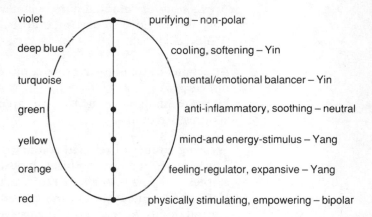

These key-phrases should be taken as pointers, not as immutable verities. Just which colours are seen to have which effects depends entirely on one's particular standpoint and orientation. Is physical, emotional, mental or spiritual health the point at issue? Or is one's main concern the experiencing and opening-up of the energy centres – the so-called chakras? Is it, indeed, merely to investigate the philosophy of colour?

You are invited to use these and all other features of this manual as a basis for learning *from your own experience*. When it comes down to it, after all, you alone have the expertise to take responsibility for your own life, manifest your own health and ultimately make sense of it all.

As we pointed out in the beginning, this summary is intended to provide an introduction to *self*-help through colour therapy. It does not rule out further research or personal practical experimentation. Nor is it any substitute for personal responsibility or free therapeutic choice – still less for seeking advice and treatment from a qualified healer wherever this is indicated.

Colour therapy techniques We have so far mentioned only *colour-irradiation*. However, a whole range of appropriate ways of applying colour are known to colour therapy. The most important of these are summarized below:

Colour-irradiation using coloured lamps
These are either used to irradiate the surface of the whole body or are targeted at specific points and areas, as already described and illustrated above. For details of one such colour-lamp, see pages 132–3.

Application of coloured film or material
This may be done to particular areas, such as the energy points (chakras).

Attachment of coloured stickers, or colouring with felt-tipped pens
Either technique may be used to target acupuncture and acupressure points.

Wearing clothes of selected colours
This applies mainly to shirts, blouses, scarves, under-clothes and possibly hats. (Take care, though, with tinted glasses and contact lenses: they can often impair the eyes' natural ability to regenerate themselves.)

Drinking colour-irradiated spring water
This may be achieved, for example, by leaving the water to stand in the sunlight for a whole day in a coloured bottle.

Deliberate choice of foods on the basis of their colour
It is known, for example, that so far as possible one should eat not just green salad, but red and yellow as well: variety of colour in food tends to result in a natural harmonization.

Free colour painting (or artistic free expression)
This enables one to see directly and to recognize one's current vibrational state of mind.

Colour visualization
This may be done either purely mentally or in meditation (see Chapter 6).

Thus, if for any reason colour-irradiation is out of the question, any of the other methods listed can be used as appropriate.

Combining healing flower essences with colour therapy

Healing flower essences and colour therapy are mutually complementary. In both cases it is the energies, or vibrational frequencies, involved that underlie the respective healing effects.

It would thus, *a priori*, be potentially revealing were one of the seven colours to correspond to each of the seven healing flower groups. Equally striking would be any correspondence to the seven major chakras, the seven rays, the Seven Stars of ancient astrology or other 'septenaries'. Practical experience has shown, however, that in certain cases a healing flower essence is best supplemented by *two different* colours.

The following correspondences between healing flower essences and colour therapy were discovered in much the same way as the assignment by Dr Bach of healing effects to the various remedies – namely as a result of personal experiment, repeated application in the context of healing practice, direct research and simple intuition.

Mutual reinforcement

One principle obtains throughout: once a given healing flower essence has been recognized as fitting the case in question, the particular colour mentioned will further reinforce the effect of that essence's harmonizing vibrations.

But the reverse is also true: once it has been established that a given colour has the desired therapeutic effect, it is recommended that the appropriate essence be administered from among the various listed healing flower essences.

Healing flower color cards

A pack of colour cards is already commercially available, showing on the front the picture of a particular healing flower and on the back the colour that corresponds to it. This 'card game' is an excellent way of finding out intuitively which vibrations one needs to reinforce and harmonize within oneself (see the detailed description on pages 127–30).

On the following pages you will see how the colours are allocated to the seven main groups of healing flower essences. (Details of a portable colour-lamp suitable for multicolour irradiation, complete with pyramid-focus, will be found on page 132.)

Group 1: 'Fear' **Healing colour: yellow**
As we have seen, the 'fear' group comprises:
Rock Rose
Mimulus

Cherry Plum
Aspen
Red Chestnut

The healing effect of all five essences is complemented by
yellow, which is always applied to the *Yin* aspect (that is,
the front) of the body.

Ideally, yellow light should be brought to bear on the
lower end of the breastbone (see illustration), as this is
where we are best able to absorb and convert yellow's
fear-dispelling qualities. To put it another way, this is the
point where we are most receptive to energies that are
suitable for balancing out fear and harmonizing it.
(Trained acupuncturists will recognize this 'alarm point'
as CV 15.)

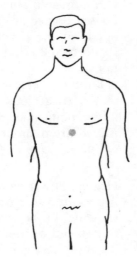

Group 2:   **Healing colours: red and green**
'Uncertainty'   The 'uncertainty' group comprises:
Cerato
Scleranthus
Gentian
Gorse
Hornbeam
Wild Oat

The vibrations of all these essences correspond to *red*,
which acts on the *front* of the body (see left-hand illustration).

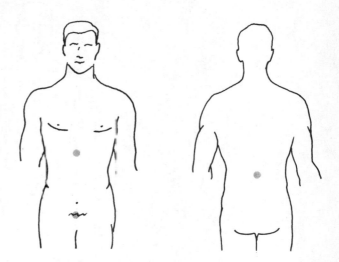

Gorse and Wild Oat work better, however, if *in these two cases* the back of the body is also irradiated with *green* (see illustration above).

Group 3: 'Not sufficient interest in present circumstances'

Healing colours: yellow and turquoise
This group comprises:
  Clematis
  Honeysuckle
  Wild Rose
  Olive
  White Chestnut
  Mustard
  Chestnut Bud

The harmonizing effects of the *first three* of these flower essences – Clematis, Honeysuckle and Wild Rose – are complemented in colour therapy by *yellow*, which is applied anywhere on the *front* of the body (no specific points are designated here). See illustration overleaf.

The vibrations of the *other four* remedies – Olive, White Chestnut, Mustard and Chestnut Bud – correspond to *turquoise*, which should be shone on the neck area (that is, the throat chakra and thyroid gland).

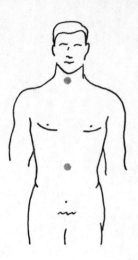

| *Group 4:* | **Healing colours: green and red** |
| *'Loneliness'* | This group comprises: |

        Water Violet
        Impatiens
        Heather

All three flower essences are complemented by *green* on the Yang side of the body, *in the middle of the back* (see illustration).

The effect of Heather is reinforced if *red* is applied to the *front* of the body.

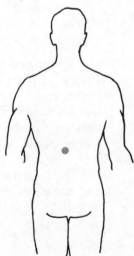

Group 5:
'Over-sensitive to
influences and
ideas'

Healing colours: blue and orange
This group comprises:
Agrimony
Centaury
Walnut
Holly

With all the remedies in Group 4, *blue* corresponds to the necessary frequency, and it is the *back* of the body (especially around the nape of the neck) that is irradiated (see illustration on the left).

If Holly is the chosen flower essence, it is helpful to apply *orange* at the centre of the upper edge of the pubic hair (see illustration on the right).

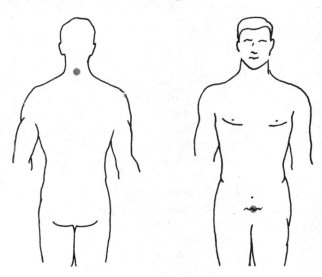

Group 6:
'Despondency or
despair'

Healing colours: orange and violet
This group comprises:
Larch
Pine
Elm
Sweet Chestnut
Star of Bethlehem
Willow
Oak
Crab Apple

The frequencies of all these essences *apart from Crab*

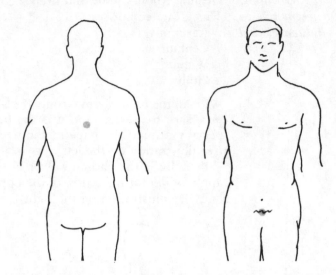

Apple correspond in terms of colour therapy to *orange*. The colour orange is beamed *onto the back between the shoulder blades* (see left-hand illustration).

In the case of Crab Apple, *violet* is applied at the centre of the upper edge of the pubic hair and on the crown centre (see right-hand illustration).

Group 7: 'Over-care for the welfare of others'

Healing colour: green
To this group belong:
  Chicory
  Vervain
  Vine
  Beech
  Rock Water

All five of these essences are effectively reinforced by *green* applied to the *back* – more or less in the middle, just above the waist (see illustration).

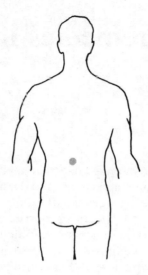

3. Natural remedies in First Aid

Basic considerations Properly applied natural remedies are of course also effective for emergencies and First Aid. *Nevertheless, in all serious emergencies the duty doctor should always be called as quickly as possible.* Often for psychological reasons as much as anything else, lay people are not always equipped to cope with emergencies, whereas the practitioner – and specifically the casualty doctor – is actually trained in how to help in such circumstances.

Our main concern here is that any treatment given should be holistic, for the simple reason that we take the world in which we live, as well as ourselves as people, to be a unity. For this reason there should never be any competition between orthodox medicine and natural healing methods, but always a sensible complementarity. Neither should there be any dogmatic exclusivity on the part of any one natural healing method vis-à-vis the others!

Holistic emergency aid In case of emergency, the following First Aid measures are intended for use until professional help arrives. They can prove useful when on holiday and far from the nearest doctor, on adventure outings or where other circumstances mean that the casualty doctor's arrival will be significantly delayed.

The great advantage of naturopathy is precisely that, in the right dosages, no harm can be done. Thus, naturopathic First Aid measures do not get in the way of subsequent medical treatment: instead, they actually open up the way to healing – and, if help is unobtainable, actually offer the sole possibility of treatment.

Our main concern in this chapter is to offer tips for coping with those more-or-less everyday *minor health problems* that demand First Aid.

On the following pages will be found a résumé of how to use various healing flower essences that are particularly helpful as First Aid in a number of critical situations in combination with homoeopathic remedies, and occasionally with colour therapy too.

Stay calm A vital part of any First Aid is to stay calm and start by establishing what is most urgent – dealing with the wounds, treating for shock, calming and soothing the patient or whatever – as well as summoning medical help as appropriate.

Among the more important of the everyday situations in which First Aid may be needed are:

injuries, cuts, open wounds
bleeding
wrenches, strains and sprains
bruises and contusions
bone fractures
burns, scalds and electric shocks
frostbite
insect stings
animal bites
sunstroke, heat-stroke and sunburn
panic and shock
rape
unconsciousness
collapse
asthma attacks

Cases of poisoning Poisoning is not a subject that can be addressed here. The causes of poisoning can be too diverse, the poisons themselves too difficult to identify and the therapies too complex. There are also a whole range of further emergencies that cannot be dealt with here, such as heart attacks and strokes. The whole area of headaches and backaches, similarly, must await a further book devoted to special colour therapies. First Aid remedy is always to be recommended, but in no way represents a treatment – though it does offer vital psychological support.

Important: Rather call the doctor once too often than once too seldom!

**First Aid
homoeopathy
supported by
healing flower
essences and
colour therapy**

*Injuries, cuts,
stabs*

First of all find out whether the wound is bleeding or needs cleaning.

It is good for minor wounds to bleed initially, so as to reduce the risk of external impurities entering the wound, as well as to minimize any danger of blood poisoning or tetanus (for *profuse* bleeding see next section). In the case of minor wounds, then, gentle pressure or massage around the injury is entirely recommended, in order to encourage initial bleeding and so promote self-cleansing.

Dirty wounds should be cleansed carefully with luke-warm **Calendula** water (never apply **Arnica** to open wounds!). To one cup of water add 7 drops of Calendula essence.

Never apply plasters or bandages to minor injuries: light, air and sunlight are much better and quicker at healing the tissues.

The following instructions for the use of healing flower essences and colour therapy apply to *all* the wounds and injuries mentioned in this section.

Healing flower essences
The **First Aid remedy** can be used both internally and externally. About 4 drops of the diluted essence should be taken on the tongue once every hour until the symptoms subside. If the stock bottle of concentrate is the only one available, 2 drops should be taken directly on the tongue, or 4 drops in a small glass of water, to be taken in sips. Externally, some 4 drops of diluted First Aid remedy may be applied to the wound itself.

In addition, around 4 drops of **Crab Apple** may be taken if one feels that either internal or external cleansing is needed (as also in the further case of suppurating wounds).

Colour therapy
Irradiation of the wound with **green** for some three or four minutes promotes healing by stimulating tissue growth.

Blue should be used for all suppurating wounds (for such purposes commercial colour therapy lamps are available, both with and without pyramid-focus – see page 132).

Homoeopathy

Note re dosage: unless otherwise indicated, *external* treatment should be continued until there is visible improvement, but *internal* treatment (indicated throughout by the words 'to be taken') should be given once only.

For *all wounds and injuries*:
Arnica 30x* in tablet form or as drops: 2 to 3 tablets or drops every hour, to be taken (internally) until the symptoms improve noticeably. Alternatively, **Arnica 200c** (in a so-called high potency, in other words), in granule form: 2 granules to be taken *once only*.

For *stab wounds, splinters* (supplementary treatment):
For dressings (that is, externally), **Ledum tincture:** 7 drops to one cup of water. For taking internally, **Ledum 200c** – for minor pricks, a single dose of 2 granules; for larger stab wounds, 2 granules every 4 hours.

In cases where such injuries involve damage to the *nerves*, **Hypericum 200c** taken internally will afford relief: 2 granules to be taken once only.

For *cuts* (supplementary treatment):
Staphisagria 30c, 2 granules to be taken every hour to quarter of an hour, until the symptoms noticeably improve.

For *splinters, thorns or prickles*:
If the foreign body cannot be removed with tweezers, cover it with sticking plaster or adhesive tape and then

---

*Translator's note: *Homoeopathic remedies are usually supplied either in decimal or in centesimal potencies. In Britain these are labelled 'x' and 'c' respectively. '30x' indicates that the substance or tincture in question has been diluted to ten times its original volume thirty times over (as well as being 'succussed', or shaken vigorously, on each occasion). The final solution, in other words, contains only one drop of the original substance or tincture in 10^{30}. '30c', by contrast, indicates a dilution of thirty times one hundredfold – giving a solution which, at 1 in 10^{60}, is far weaker, yet is held homoeopathically to be far more potent than the 30x potency.*

It may sometimes be necessary to order directly from sources such as Ainsworth's Homoeopathic Pharmacy, 38 New Cavendish Street, London W1M 7LH (tel. 071 935 5330), A. Nelson & Co. Ltd., 5 Endeavour Way, Wimbledon, London SW19 9UH (tel. 071 629 3118), or Weleda (UK) Ltd., Heanor Road, Ilkeston, Derbyshire (tel. 0602 309319). For most practical purposes the word 'tablets' (lactose-based) may be freely substituted for 'granules' (sucrose-based) throughout, except where a homoeopathic healer prescribes otherwise. Recommended dosages are as described in the text: directions are also given on the product label and/or the associated literature published by the manufacturers.

lift. If neither this nor a warm, soapy bath succeeds in removing it, apply **Silicea ointment 6x** or **12x** or **Hypericum oil** (St John's Wort oil) externally.

For *all suppurating wounds* (supplementary treatment): **Hepar sulph. 200c:** 3 granules to be taken two or three times within 24 hours. Also see **No. 3 tissue-salt Calc. Sulph. 6x:** 4 tablets to be sucked three times a day (see p. 99).

In addition, if the wound exudes pus after the foreign body has been removed, or if the suppuration has itself expelled it, take 3 granules of **Silicea 200c** two to three times within 24 hours.

Bleeding   Here we are concerned with bleeding from minor wounds (such as abrasions), bleeding from open lacerations and cuts, bleeding after dental extractions, nosebleeds, and bleeding associated with special circumstances or with bodily symptoms such as physical weakness after prolonged bleeding, or simple loss of blood (as in menstruation, for example).

As a general rule, bleeding from wounds should not be regarded in a negative light, but as something both useful and important. It is, after all, nature's way of cleansing the wound.

Warning: In all cases where bleeding is particularly profuse, or refuses to stop, the duty doctor must be summoned.

(If bright red blood comes out in spurts, an artery has been severed. It is then *absolutely essential* to fetch medical help or rush the patient to hospital, whilst applying a tourniquet or simple pressure above the wound as appropriate. In this event the homoeopathically trained practitioner will administer **Ipecacuanha 200c** – *purely in order to tide the patient over* – especially where nausea, shortness of breath or cold sweats also occur.)

We are unable to offer recommendations here for the use of natural remedies as First Aid in connection with internal bleeding, bleeding (suspected or otherwise) associated with fractures, or other indeterminate forms of bleeding (after accidents, for example). It is essential to have such injuries attended to and treated by competent, medically qualified experts. (Internal bleeding can be recognized by the fact that the blood pressure falls, while the pulse becomes rapid, thin, irregular and almost too weak to feel. Other indicators are restlessness; thirst; weakness; feelings of faintness; a cold, moist skin; enlarged pupils; great anxiety; and shallow, irregular breathing. Only where internal bleeding results from head-injuries is the pulse *slow* and weak.)

Healing flower essences
For *all types of bleeding* (as in all emergencies generally): **First Aid remedy** (internally only): 4 drops of the diluted remedy to be taken on the tongue every 10 minutes until the bleeding lessens or stops.

Warning: *On no account should the First Aid remedy be seen here as a direct means of stopping the bleeding. It is merely a supplementary aid to help put the patient in a more positive frame of mind, so that the healing powers of the psyche may be activated.*

Homoeopathy
The blood-staunching remedy *par excellence* is **Arnica**. It should be taken internally, never applied externally.

For *all cases of bleeding*:
Arnica 200c, to be taken internally: in case of severe injury, 2 granules to be taken every 15 to 30 minutes until the bleeding lessens; otherwise 2 to 3 granules once to three times within 24 hours. (Arnica encourages the wound to heal, helps the flow of bood to stop more quickly, and also minimizes scarring.)

For *bleeding after dental extractions involving surgery*, as well as for *jaw operations*:
Arnica 30x and **Staphisagria 30x** mixed together in drop form: 5 to 7 drops to be taken every 15 to 30 minutes on the first day: from the second day, 10 drops three times a day if the bleeding continues.

In addition, external irradiation with **green** on the affected place has shown itself to be a useful colour therapy for encouraging wounds to heal.

Nosebleeds that arise spontaneously, and are not caused by physical injury, are indicators of circulation blockages within the body that are in urgent need of expert treatment. As a general principle, the nose should first be allowed one chance to bleed; but if the nosebleed goes on for too long, two homoeopathic remedies for stopping it may be considered:

Hamamelis 200c, to be taken internally for *slow, long-lasting, thin* nosebleeds that refuse to clot: 2 to 3 granules to be taken every 15 to 30 minutes until the bleeding slows or stops.

Ferrum Phos. 200c, to be taken as above for *profuse, bright red nosebleeds.*

For *profuse, bright-red bleeding resulting from a fall from a considerable height* (regardless of whether the bleeding is external or internal – including cases where internal bleeding is suspected, as possibly indicated by the spitting or coughing up of bright-red blood), **Millefolium 200c**: 2 to 3 granules to be taken every 15 to 30 minutes (depending on the severity of the injury), or three times within 24 hours.

In classical homoeopathy, **Arnica** (the general remedy for bleeding and injuries: see above) is given internally first of all: *and only then* **Millefolium**.

In addition, if the patient has *fallen on his or her back* and is in pain, **Hypericum 200c**: 2 to 3 granules to be taken two to three times within 24 hours.

For *physical weakness as a result of prolonged loss of blood* (as, for example, in some cases of menstruation): If the loss of blood has been slow, and the patient has already become weak, **China 200c**: 2 to 3 granules to be taken one to three times every 24 hours until he or she feels stronger.

If the loss of blood has been very rapid and the patient is consequently pale and totally exhausted, **Trillium 200c**: to be taken internally, as per China 200c above.

Wrenches, sprains and strains

Damp compresses, moistened with Calendula water (cold or warm according to the patient's preference) have proved a valuable home remedy for easing pain and reducing swelling.

For this purpose, 1 teaspoonful of **Calendula essence** (available from the chemist) should be diluted in 1 cupful of water.

Healing flower essences
Of the healing flower essences, the **First Aid remedy** (taken internally) is, as usual, to be recommended; also,

for wrenches, sprains and strains, **First Aid remedy cream**. Take 4 drops of the diluted essence either directly or in water; or gently rub in the cream two or three times a day until the condition improves.

Colour therapy
Supplementary colour therapy consists in irradiating the affected part with **green** (without pyramid-focus) for 20 minutes or so three or more times a day.

Schüssler tissue-salts
Calc. Fluor. 12x, taken internally: 3 tablets to be sucked every hour until improvement is apparent.

Homoeopathy
For all wrenches, sprains and strains, **Arnica 200c** should be taken internally: 2 to 3 granules daily until the condition improves.

If the joint or other affected part gets hot, swells up and becomes painful – and/or if there is a 'grating' feeling the moment it is touched, and the condition improves with movement – **Rhus. tox. 200c**: 2 granules to be taken every 2 hours until improvement occurs.

If the joint swells up and hurts with the slightest movement, **Bryonia 200c** should also be taken: 2 granules to be taken three times within 24 hours.

If the swelling is not the main concern, but the patient wants to lie down – yet this makes the condition worse, while movement brings no improvement either – **Ruta 200c** should be administered internally: 2 granules to be taken three times within 24 hours.

If the swelling is severe, the joint is cold and numb and a cold compress brings some improvement, **Ledum 200c** should also be given: 2 granules to be taken three times within 24 hours.

If the swelling does not go down and water seems to be accumulating around the joint – as also in cases of bursitis – **Apis 200c**: 2 granules to be taken one to three times within 24 hours, or ditto for up to 3 days.

Bruises Bruises are injuries that affect the soft tissues (not the bones) beneath the skin without producing open wounds.

Healing flower essences
As in all cases of First Aid, **First Aid remedy** and **First Aid remedy cream** should be used: for dosage, see the section on injuries etc. on page 70.

Colour therapy
Blue, and possibly also **green,** are effective as colour treatments: irradiate locally without pyramid-focus for 20 minutes several times a day until detectable relief is obtained.

Homoeopathy
The principle remedy is once again **Arnica 200c** taken internally: 2 granules to be taken one or more times (depending on the degree of pain) within 24 hours.

For bruising of the fingers, toes, spine, coccyx, palms or soles of the feet, or for black eyes – whether as a result of hammer blows, falling over, getting fingers jammed in doors, knocking into things, getting the feet trodden on while dancing or whatever – **Hypericum 200c** should be taken in addition: 2 granules to be taken one or more times within 24 hours, depending on the severity of the pain.

For bruising of the genitals – after such things as rape, cycling and sporting accidents, for example – women and girls should also take **Staphisagria 200c:** 2 granules to be taken every 15 minutes to once every 4 hours, according to the intensity of the injury and damage. In similar cases men and boys should take **Argentum metallicum 200c:** 2 granules to be taken every 15 minutes initially, then every 4 hours as the condition improves. If the bruises to the genitals are also bleeding, though, both sexes should be given **Phosphorus 200c** first, *before* either the Staphisagria or the Argentum: 2 granules to be taken every 15 minutes until the bleeding has stopped.

In all the cases mentioned expert medical help should be sought.

Fractures   If a bone fracture has occurred, or even if it is merely suspected, a doctor should of course be consulted, or the duty doctor summoned.

Instructions for proper care until the doctor can treat the injury are given at First Aid courses, and can also be found in relevant books and leaflets.

It is well known that one of the most important things to do is to take care to keep the patient still so that all movement is avoided; judicious splinting may also be needed, as also may the cooling of whichever part of the body is hurting (with ice, for example).

Naturopathic remedies are no replacement for medical treatment or surgical intervention. Used as First Aid, however, they can have a favourable effect on the patient's state of mind and thus on his or her powers of self-healing.

Tissue salts
For the use of **Calc. Fluor.** and **Calc. Phos.** to underpin the healing process, see the later section entitled *Essential mineral salts for the maintenance of our health* (which starts on page 93).

Healing flower essences
The right vibration heals! The notion applies here, too – in this case to the **First Aid remedy**, which can be most helpful in counteracting the shock of the event. First Aid remedy drops only: 4 drops of the diluted remedy to be taken on the tongue every 10 minutes until the shock has clearly subsided.

Homoeopathy
Once again **Arnica 200c**, taken internally, is the remedy of first choice: 2 granules to be taken once only.

Thereafter, any pains that arise can be soothed and made generally more bearable with **Symphytum 200c**: 2 granules to be taken once only.

Burns, scalds and electric shocks
Burns are categorized according to the degree of burning and the size of the skin area affected.

The severity of a burn is measured not so much in terms of how deeply the damage has penetrated into the tissues, as of how extensive the affected skin area is.

It should be borne in mind that burns affecting more than 10% of the body's total surface area are by definition severe and may well be dangerous, even if the skin itself is only slightly burned.

The degree of burning is normally determined thus:
First degree: red or discoloured skin.

Second degree: heat blisters as well as red or discoloured skin.

Third degree: charring of the entire skin surface.

Warning: Never smear fatty substances or ointments on
burns!

Healing flower essences
In view of the fact that a burn always entails some kind of
shock, the **First Aid remedy** drops should always be
given: 4 drops of the solution (or of the neat essence if
need be) to be taken on the tongue every 10 minutes for
an hour.

Colour therapy
Extensive irradiation of the affected places with **blue** will
at very least prove capable of soothing the pain and
promoting healing. Indeed, colour therapy using blue has
been known to produce near-miraculous healing effects
entirely unaided. Reports from the USA tell of how an
eight-year-old girl with third-degree burns was taken to a
colour therapy clinic in California, where she was treated
with blue light and made a total recovery.

Homoeopathy
First of all **Arnica 200c**, to be taken internally: one dose
of 2 granules. At the same time **Aconite 200c**: 2 granules
to be taken every 15 minutes until the shock has subsided.

By way of external treatment, naturopathic experience
suggests either using **undiluted vinegar** (preferably fruit
vinegar) or the application of cloths soaked in it. This is
the quickest way to get rid of the pain and the best way to
encourage healing – and there are no scars, either. Use
warm or very warm water only if no vinegar is available:
cold water may admittedly deaden the nerves and thus
temporarily dull any sensitivity to pain, but it also slows
down the body's self-healing processes, the pain can
under certain circumstances return in even more acute
form, and infections can occur. If charred clothing is
sticking to the burn or scald, it should be soaked in
vinegar and then carefully pulled off: bring in the doctor
if necessary. Pure **Aloe Vera Gel** may be carefully applied
to the burnt areas. (In the United States pure Aloe Vera
Gel is not only used externally for burns, but also for

sunburn, as well as for speeding up the healing of wounds and minor injuries. It is also diluted with spring water and taken internally as a gargle for small injuries in the area of the mouth and jaw, as well as being drunk in order to soothe and heal irritated stomach and gut mucosa.)

In addition to Arnica and Aconite, the following should be taken internally:

for *very severe pain,* **Causticum 200c**: 2 granules to be taken every 15 minutes until the pain has subsided.

for *sharp, burning pain from blisters or burns,* **Cantharis 200c** dosage as for Causticum 200c.

Severe burns

Warning: If the burns are severe, or cover more than about 10% of the body area – 1% corresponds more or less to the back of the hand – either a doctor or a hospital must be sought at all costs.

For *burns resulting from electric shocks* (lightning strikes, mains shocks – for example, in the bath)

 – first switch off the source of the electricity (hair dryer, electric fence or whatever), taking care to avoid coming into contact with it yourself,
 – then treat and care for the patient as described above.

   If the breathing has stopped, or in the event of unconsciousness or apparent death

 – as ever, first switch off the source of electricity, while taking care not to come into contact with it yourself,
 – call the doctor immediately, and in the meantime
 – wet the lips every 15 minutes with drops of **Nux vomica 200c** (if necessary, dissolve 2 granules in a little liquid).

If the face has turned blue, additionally give **Lachesis 200c** in the same way as Nux vomica.

First Aid remedy drops will assist in harmonizing the psychological shock.

Frostbite The greatest danger in serious cases of frostbite is that all sensitivity to cold is lost – since the cold deadens the nerves – and the patient is unaware of just how 'frozen stiff' the limbs or body have become.

Careless movements or contacts can then easily lead to

ruptures or fractures, whether of the nose, ears, fingers or toes.

Homoeopathy
External treatment:
Rub snow or ice gently into the frozen places: if available, mix **Camphor Mother Tincture** with the ice-water (from a few drops to a tablespoonful, depending on the size of the area affected).
Internal treatment:
Camphor Mother Tincture: 7 drops to be diluted in a glass of water and sipped slowly.

If, once the affected part has been revived, *severe pain* is experienced, **Carbo vegetabilis 200c** should be administered: 2 granules to be taken every 4 hours until the pain subsides.

If Carbo vegetabilis fails to help and the pain is still severe and burning, **Arsenicum album 200c** should be used: dosage as for Carbo vegetabilis.

If the person giving the treatment experiences severe pain of his or her own while rubbing in the snow or ice, he or she should also take Arsenicum album.

Healing flower essences
Here, once again **First Aid remedy** in drop form can also provide additional help. Normal dosage: 4 drops of the solution to be given on the tongue every 10 minutes until improvement is experienced.

Colour therapy
Orange is recommended as a colour therapy, rather than the perhaps too intensive red, though admittedly we have no documented evidence on this.

Insect stings   Recommended for the external treatment of all insect stings is the rubbing in of **First Aid remedy**
For *mosquito and horsefly bites*:
    if severely itchy or burning, **Ledum 200c**: 2 granules to be taken one to three times within 24 hours;
    if they refuse to go down and cause ulcerous swellings, **Carbolicum acidum 200c**: dosage as for Ledum 200c.

With *bee stings*, the first thing to do is to remove the sting (if it is still sticking in the skin). Then apply the familiar household remedy cf wetting the affected spot and dabbing **common salt** on it. In addition, **Apis 200c** should be taken internally: 2 granules to be taken once only.

With *wasp and hornet stings*, once again start by removing any sting, then dab on moist common salt and supplement with **Vespa 200c**: 2 granules to be taken once only.

Should there be an allergic reaction to bee, wasp or hornet stings, such stings can pose a serious danger to life. Symptoms indicating this are (among others) mental confusion; faintness and restlessness; difficulty in breathing; bluish skin colour (not necessarily around the affected part itself); coughing; headaches; and possibly unconsciousness. **In such cases seek a doctor at once.** In the meantime give **Arsenicum album 200c** internally: 2 granules, initially once every 2 hours; thereafter, reduce the dosage to once every 4 hours until the state of shock has subsided.

Should the allergic reaction lead to *heart problems*, with the face turning bluish and the area of the sting also showing a blue discolouration, supplement with **Lachesis 200c**: 2 granules to be taken once a day.

In the case of *tick bites* it needs to be borne in mind that there is a risk (albeit not universally agreed on) that they may be a vehicle for disease-transmission, as well as a possible cause of meningitis. In case of uncertainty, then, it is best to seek the advice of a qualified physician. On no account should any attempt be made to pull out the tick by brute force. The head of the tick should be sealed off from the air with oil or glue. The tick will then release its grip, and after a short while it will come out quite easily.

To prevent meningitis after a tick bite, **tick bite fever nosode 200x** should be taken internally: 2 granules to be taken once only. (Experienced homoeopaths will also be familiar with the use of this remedy against the possible consequences of allopathic tick inoculations.) In addition, **Ledum 200c** should be taken internally: 2 granules to be taken once only.

First Aid remedy cream has likewise proved valuable as a supplementary treatment for tick bites.

Animal bites If one has been bitten by a generally unaggressive wild animal, or by a normally tame, but now aggressive domestic pet (or even if one has come into contact with the spittle of such an animal), an anti-rabies injection is indicated. In this case seek a doctor immediately.

A general point about animal bites is that bacteria can enter the wound, from which it is then very difficult to remove them. For this reason the bite should first of all be vigorously massaged so as to promote sufficient bleeding to encourage the wound to cleanse itself.

Healing flower essences
Here again, as in all emergencies, **First Aid remedy** should be taken internally: 4 drops of the solution (or, if necessary, of the pure essence) to be taken every hour.

Homoeopathy
Arnica 200c: 2 granules to be taken internally every 15 minutes until the shock has subsided.

Ledum 200c is the chief remedy for bites: 2 granules to be taken internally one to three times within 24 hours.

If *nerve pains* occur, add **Hypericum 200c**: dosage as for Ledum 200c.

If there is a threat of *blood-poisoning* – recognizable by (among other things) a red streak extending from the wound towards the heart – add **Gunpowder 3x or 6x**: 6 granules to be taken every hour at first, then every 3 hours.

For **Rabies**, pending treatment by a doctor, **Lyssinum 1000c**: 2 doses of 2 granules to be taken at an interval of 5 minutes.

For *bites from spiders, snakebite and scorpion stings*, homoeopathic remedies are given according to the symptomatology outlined below.

In all cases of venomous bites and stings, a doctor or hospital should always be located as quickly as possible.

Among the household remedies applicable until expert treatment arrives are **ice packs** applied to the injury in order to slow or impede the spread of the poison: **lancing** and/or careful, generalized, 'one-way massage' to squeeze the poison away from the heart and towards the wound; and, in the event of a limb being affected, the application of a **ligature** above the wound.

Travellers in regions where such risks are present are recommended to equip themselves with the following homoeopathic remedies beforehand, in order to be able to treat any animal bites homoeopathically:

- to speed up healing and treat shock in all cases, **Arnica 200c:** 2 granules to be taken internally once only.
- to strengthen resistance, and in the event of redness and discolouration around a bite or incipient risk of blood-poisoning and infection (indeed, generally), **Echinacea 200c:** 2 granules to be taken internally three times a day (or, if necessary, 10 to 20 drops of the Mother Tincture every hour), until the patient feels noticeably better or the relevant medical treatment can be set in train.
- for bites that have turned dark red or dark blue, and from which dark red blood may be oozing, with the symptoms worsening after sleep, add **Lachesis 200c:** 2 granules to be taken internally every 30 minutes until the discolouration disappears or expert treatment arrives.
- for dark-red discolouration of the face, but with paleness about the nose and mouth, severe exhaustion and a heightened sense of smell, **Carbolicum acidum 200c:** dosage as for Lachesis 200c above.
- for severe swelling and discolouration around the bite, for rattlesnake bites and in cases of cardiac insufficiency with a tendency to collapse, as well as where the onset of the symptoms is rapid and they are worsened by jolting, **Crotalus 200c:** dosage as for Lachesis 200c above.
- if the wound feels cold and numb, acute pain and violent shivering occur, and the condition worsens at the slightest touch or merely on thinking about the situation, **Oxalicum acidum 200c:** dosage as for Lachesis 200c above.

Sunstroke, heatstroke and sunburn

The typical symptoms of sunstroke are headaches, dizziness and weakness, feelings of faintness up to and including actual unconsciousness, possible breathing problems, bodily pains and vomiting, and occasionally even feelings of 'not being all there' mentally. In cases of heatstroke there will also be a high body temperature.

Sunstroke and heatstroke normally occur because the body cannot get rid of its heat through sweating.

(For simple *sunburn* see the detailed advice given at the

end of this section: for *collapse* see the relevant section on page 90.)

General First Aid Treatment
- Drink plenty of fluids, preferably hot(!), so as to encourage sweating.
- Administer salt as the symptoms arise, so as to ease sweating, since sweating has a cooling effect (exception: extreme sweating while working in extreme heat, as for example in blast furnaces, mines and the tropics).
- Seek a cool (but not cold) environment.
- If necessary lie down flat, with the head slightly raised.

Healing flower essences
Add **First Aid remedy** drops to drinking fluids: 4 drops of the essence per glass, to be sipped slowly.

Colour therapy
Wear as much **blue** as possible on and around the body: also use blue for irradiating the whole body and/or the head. Similarly, wrap the head in a damp, blue cloth, and/or lay a blue cloth over the body if irradiation with blue is not possible.

Homoeopathy
If the head is red, hot and steaming, with wide pupils, as well as with strongly pulsating veins in the neck and dryness of skin, **Belladonna 200c**: 2 granules to be dissolved in a glass of warm fluid and drunk in sips. If necessary, repeat until better.

Where there is a threat of unconsciousness or a raging headache, and the feeling that the skull is 'too big' or about to burst; where the head symptoms get worse with the slightest jolt; where there is a feeling that one cannot lie down because 'the pillow is throbbing too much'; where severe pain is experienced on bending the head back; where the eyes are dull and glassy and the skin is dry, **Glonoinum 200c**: 2 granules to be taken once only.

If the patient has fallen asleep in the sun, feels ill on waking and sick as soon as he or she attempts to get up; if the face is pale as death and the skin is dry, **Aconite 200c**:

2 granules to be taken once. If necessary, repeat once only half-an-hour later.

If the patient is quite obviously shivery and weak, severe dizziness and faintness have set in and the eyelids seem too heavy to keep open, **Gelsemium 200c**: 2 granules to be taken every 30 minutes until the symptoms improve noticeably.

Where the patient is mentally vague to the point of confusion; in cases of throbbing, pulsating or hammering headache (with any tendency to nosebleed easing the headache), **Melilotus 200c**: 2 granules to be taken once.

Sunburn

The rubbing in of pure (**fruit**) **vinegar** has proved its worth as a home remedy for sunburn. In the USA especially, pure **Aloe Vera Gel** is also used.

The **First Aid remedy cream**, applied sparingly, can also help.

Panic and shock Panic and shock are familiar side-effects not only of accidents and severe injuries, but also of sudden psychological traumas and misfortunes. In this section we shall merely be addressing the question of how to cope with the state of psychological shock and treat it naturopathically, not with the care and healing of the physical causes and symptoms themselves. (If panic and shock lead to unconsciousness, see the next section.)

Panic or shock can occur as a result of car or bicycle accidents, falls from horses, into water and so on, and physical attacks including rape. Rows, dismissal from work, bad news, upsetting letters, shouting matches involving infants and children – to say nothing of extreme or destructive music, bad school reports and so on – can likewise lead to states of panic or shock.

In fact anything whatever that happens very suddenly or violently – even joyful events – can set off an attack of panic or shock in particularly sensitive people.

Healing flower essences

The **First Aid remedy** has proved its worth as a universal treatment for panic and shock. This particular essence, whether in diluted or undiluted form, should always be kept to hand – in the handbag, in the car, in the briefcase or wherever.

The First Aid remedy has a direct harmonizing effect on the vibrational state of body, mind and soul when the physical organism has come into more or less extreme disharmony with its own soul as a result of some sudden, violent event.

We would recall the reader's attention at this point to the interrelationships already explained in our first chapter.

Our soul, our Self – the divine spark that is our very innermost nature – is of course always 'whole', always complete, always healthy. In Edward Bach's view, illness arises only as and when we no longer allow our personality to be guided by the soul in all its perfection, but instead follow the inspiration of the ego. From this point on, the personality no longer resonates with the soul. If we then ignore this dissonance, the soul proceeds to use physical disease symptoms to force us to come to grips with it.

In cases of panic or shock, such dissonances are imposed upon our personality from 'out there' (always assuming, that is, we do not acknowledge at this point that there may be self-imposed, 'karmic' reasons for encountering the situations that shock us). It is then our job to sort out how to harmonize our externally imposed state of panic or shock, by bringing our personality back into accord with the primal, perfect, creative resonance of the soul.

This is precisely the point that the First Aid remedy addresses. It mediates the influence of the subtle harmonic vibrations of five mutually tuned healing flowers on the so-called aura – which not only envelops us, but also radiates from within, as though from 'inside us' – in such a way as to raise our personal state of consciousness. People who are intuitively aware are able to perceive this change of resonance directly, at the very moment of taking the First Aid remedy drops.

In cases of panic and shock, then, it is once again a case of **First Aid remedy**: 4 drops to 1 glass of water, to be sipped slowly once every hour until the condition has passed.

Should the condition reappear later – including in dreams, for example – take First Aid remedy again (see below for further homoeopathic remedies). Since what is at issue is vibrational energies, not material substances, 4 drops of the solution are just as effective as 4 drops of the undiluted essence.

Homoeopathy

For *shock arising from panic*; quivering with fear; wide, frightened eyes, with great anxiety and disquiet; a desire to jump up, accompanied by giddiness, followed by a wish to lie down and fear of getting up again; and/or the threat of fright-induced miscarriage – **Aconite 200c**: 2 granules to be taken one to three times within one day.

For *shock arising from injury*, plus possible over-sensitivity of the whole body leading to avoidance of contact, the wish to be left alone and a tendency to play down the whole situation – **Arnica 200c**, to be taken internally. Dosage as for Aconite 200c above.

For *shock arising from bad news*, with extreme weakness, often accompanied by uncontrollable shaking – **Gelsemium 200c**: dosage as for Aconite 200c above.

For *panic or shock as a result of joy* (that is, exaggerated emotional excitement as a result of positive events and conditions); and for violent attacks of laughing and crying leading to internal collapse – **Coffea 200c**: dosage as for Aconite 200c above. (In emergency, the smell or even a few sips of ordinary strong coffee can also help.)

If the panic and shock lead to *residual fear* or *screaming fits*, or *where the patient keeps repeating the same sentence over and over again*; also where extreme apathy sets in and neither Arnica nor Aconite seem to do the state of shock any good – **Opium 200c**: 2 granules to be taken once only.

Warning: Although Opium 200c is a strictly homoeopathic remedy, it may well be found that it is available only on prescription. Where this is the case – as in Germany, for example – the double standards of state-regulated health provision are of course clearly exposed to view. In a homoeopathic dilution of 200c, after all, there is not a single molecule of opium remaining – once again, in other words, it is a case of the *vibration* doing the healing. Nevertheless this remedy is not generally available in Germany – indeed, it was by law not even available to healers until just a few years back.

This naturally poses certain questions of those who see fit to play politics with our health. If homoeopathy 'doesn't work', how is it that this remedy – along with others such as Radium bromatum 200c – is not generally available? If, on the other hand, homoeopathy *does* work, why are more and more legal hurdles constantly being placed in the way of patients and healers alike in an effort to stop them using homoeopathy and thus producing savings for the health insurance?

Rape   Rape, alas, is still far too often played down as though it were relatively unimportant. Neither (man-made) laws nor (male) medicine and psychology have so far done anything like justice to the sheer brutality involved in sexual oppression and exploitation (not least, as is well known, within marriage). Even today, the woman has to start off by allowing herself to be subjected to the most embarrassing and shocking investigations and interrogations. *She* is the one who is supposed to reproach herself for any possible 'feelings of enjoyment': she it is who has to put up with any number of further debasements and humiliations.

Rape is all too commonly seen by male-dominated society as a mere peccadillo – unless, of course, it is a European woman who happens to be raped by a 'guest worker', or a white woman by a black. Then, of course, the whole structure of society as we know it is suddenly in mortal jeopardy.

There are now self-help organizations to support female rape victims, but all those who are active in the healing profession, whether they be women or men, should be aware of their special responsibility for supporting women as they undergo the relevant medical examinations, as well as for protecting them from further psychological after-effects and for offering them back-up and support during police investigations or in court.

The conduct of medics, psychologists, lawyers and others vis-à-vis such women as are involved is a direct reflection of their own state of consciousness – and not least where their reaction is merely to play the whole thing down as a matter of minor consequence.

Homoeopathy
Apart from **Aconite 200c** and **Arnica 200c** (for the symptoms already described in earlier sections), treatment may also involve the following:

for *violent physical injuries,* such as pulled or torn tissues, ruptures and so on, **Staphisagria 200c**: 2 granules to be taken one to three times within 24 hours.

for *persistent or severe psychological trauma,* **Sepia 200c**: dosage as for Staphisagria 200c above.

for *deep, recurrent worry and grief* resulting from the rape (as well as where a partnership breaks up as an indirect consequence of it), and where this persists like a thorn in the side, accompanied by deep sighing – **Ignatia 200c**: dosage as for Staphisagria 200c above.

Fainting Before panic and shock have a chance to lead to acute unconsciousness, the instructions listed in the earlier section should be followed.

If the unconsciousness persists – longer than a few minutes, that is – a trained physician must be called at all costs. Anyone who suffers regular fainting fits should visit the practitioner at his or her clinic.

In cases of unconsciousness, the regular access of oxygen to the brain is impeded or even interrupted. The patient is 'laid low' because nature obliges us to take up the most favourable position for increasing the flow of oxygen to the brain.

First Aid

The vital *external* First Aid treatments are:
- Lay the patient on the floor or a couch, preferably in a stable position on his or her side, and in any case with the head turned to one side (in case of vomiting).
- If there is reddening of the face, raise the head higher.
- Loosen the clothing so as not to impede the breathing or circulation.
- Massage the feet vigorously with the shoes removed, pressing the toes (or at least the tips of the toes) hard against the balls of the feet.
- Press hard with the fingertip or fingernail – or with a ball-point pen or similar – on the point just underneath the root of the nose, between the nose and the upper lip.
- Sprinkle cold water on the face, the temples and the nape of the neck.

- Massage the back of the hand between the ring and little fingers.
- Hold a bottle of smelling salts (camphor, or failing that perfume, as well as First Aid remedy) underneath the nose.
- Trickle First Aid remedy onto the lips: 4 drops every 5 minutes.

Homoeopathy
Treat *according to the precipitating cause of the unconsciousness*, as follows:

From *suffocatingly hot rooms*, or equally from *packed crowds and get-togethers*, **Pulsatilla 200c**: 2 granules to be taken once only.

From *panic and shock*, **Aconite 200c**: 2 granules to be taken once only. Where the breath is actually rattling, **Opium 200c**: 2 granules to be taken once only (this may not be freely available other than on prescription – see page 87).

From *extreme vexation and/or really severe pain*, **Chamomilla 200c**: 2 granules to be taken once only.

From *excessive joy* (at winning at bingo, receiving a legacy or whatever) or *excessive emotional excitement* (gripping sports events, erotic situations and so on), **Coffea 200c**: 2 granules to be taken once only. If necessary, ordinary coffee may also be trickled onto a cloth or handkerchief and held under the nose (also useful just before a fainting fit sets in).

From *bad news while in an extremely weak state*, possibly leading to involuntary urination or defecation while unconscious, **Gelsemium 200c**: 2 granules to be taken once only.

From *alcohol-, nicotine-* or *drug-abuse, sexual excesses, over-exertion and prolonged lack of sleep, oversensitivity to smells and tobacco smoke*, **Nux vomica 200c**: 2 granules to be taken once only.

From *severe loss of blood* (as in cases of injury, accident, operation, unusually severe menstrual bleeding, miscarriage and so on) and consequent weakness, **China 200c**: 2 granules to be taken once only.

Collapse   Collapse can be seen as a manifestation of severe enfeeblement. It is a breakdown that stops just short of unconsciousness: in other words, the patient is still 'there', but hardly in a fit state to be talked to. A collapse always signifies a failure of life energy.

(While there may be various causes of a collapse, it should never be confused with a heart-attack. Heart attacks are normally presaged by 'warning signs', such as sudden pains emanating from the heart, possibly radiating outwards into the left shoulder and arm, the stomach area or the neck. Though homoeopathy can admittedly help here, too, self-treatment is under no circumstances to be recommended. *In cases of heart attack, always seek or call expert medical help.*)

Homoeopathy

Where there is a cold sweat affecting the whole body *and* the body itself is cold – with an abnormal craving for air (the patient actually wants air fanned into his or her face), *cold* and *shallow* breathing, cold knees and a sunken, yellowish-green face – **Carbo vegetabilis 200c:** 2 granules to be taken one to three times within 24 hours.

Where the patient is icy-cold to the point of turning blue – with the blood feeling as though it has turned to ice in the veins, the breath coming in *deep* gasps, weakness as a result of severe loss of fluids, and diarrhoea as a result of intestinal illness, also involving cramps in the legs – **Veratrum album 200c:** dosage as for Carbo vegetabilis above.

As ever, **First Aid remedy** is also to be recommended: 4 drops (diluted or undiluted) to be trickled onto the lips every 15 minutes until there is an improvement.

Asthma attacks Asthma requires treatment by a trained practitioner. It is perfectly amenable to healing using natural methods, provided that the therapist has sufficient experience at his or her disposal, and that the patient is prepared to examine and change his or her psychosomatic attitudes to life. Asthma is often called 'the weeping of the soul' – weeping, that is, over unconquered fears and inhibitions, many of them not of the patient's own making.

Asthmatic attacks can be eased by certain homoeopathic remedies. But for severe attacks, which can lead to actual suffocation, the doctor must be summoned.

The **First Aid remedy** will once again prove soothing: 4 drops to be trickled onto the lips. The chest can also be rubbed with **First Aid remedy cream.**

Often, too, a particular body position can ease the breathing: this involves kneeling on the floor in the Muslim prayer position, with the top half of the body prostrate on the floor and the arms stretched forwards.

Homoeopathy
Once again, the treatment depends on the symptoms.

If the patient is suffering from *asthmatic shortness of breath*
- and is at the same time suffering from fear and anxiety, or where a suffocating feeling is experienced shortly after midnight and the patient is therefore reluctant to go to bed, **Arsenicum album 200c**: 2 granules to be taken once only, or once every 15 minutes until medical help can be sought.
- and, after spasmodic coughing, the attack is accompanied by retching or vomiting, and eating and talking makes matters worse – with the symptoms worse in the evening than in the morning – **Carbo vegetabilis 200c**: dosage as above.
- and spasmodic coughing leads to a danger of suffocation, often with vomiting and the body almost blue with cold, as well as violent, cutting pains in the stomach or intestines, with the coughing and retching being eased by cold drinks, but all the symptoms being made worse by touching – as well as in cases of convulsions and epileptic fits – **Cuprum 200c**: 2 granules to be taken one to three times within 24 hours until medical treatment can be given.
- and the patient is suffering from a feeling of pressure on the chest, and constantly has to cough as though in gasps, with a fear of suffocation, plus retching without actual expectoration, **Ipecacuanha 200c**: dosage as above.

If none of the above remedies proves capable of bringing relief, **Aconite 200c** should be considered for its ability to remove or ease anxiety states (in the case of asthma attacks, arising from feelings of suffocation).

4. Homoeopathic tissue-salts to complement the healing flower essences

Essential mineral salts for the maintenance of our health

What is to be done when a system breaks down? We could take a particular case by way of illustration. A major steel manufacturer, say, is threatened with collapse. Workers have to be laid off, the tax yield and gross national product both decline, the whole economy suffers. What to do? There are demands for subsidies, even though experience shows that, far from putting matters right, all they do is stave off disaster for a while.

Another example, this time rather nearer to the matter at hand, is that of agriculture. Thanks to 'modern' farming techniques, artificial fertilizers, mass production and so on, we have managed to create a more 'productive' food industry. But what is the result? Thousands of small farmers go bankrupt, and the agricultural industry has to be propped up with billions of pounds in subsidies. And instead of being offered a rich variety of natural *food*stuffs to buy, we have to put up with a relatively limited range of *fillers* that are for the most part deficient in both nutritional value and smell.

As a result, health-conscious shoppers attempt to offset this lack by patronizing wholefood and health food outlets, and by going out of their way to take supplementary vitamins, minerals, plant juices and restorative tonics. This may appear to be a sensible way out of the problem – but in reality it is merely yet another kind of 'subsidy'.

Inner reinforcement

What we know in economic terms as a 'subsidy' may be likened to what in health circles is known as the *substitution principle*. Once a system becomes incapable of standing on its own two feet, assistance is drafted in from outside – in the case of the economy in the form of taxpayers' money, and in the case of the human body in the form of substitutes and supplements.

The problem is of course that the subsidies soon become used up, the replacement materials exhausted – and still there is a lack of any incentive for the system to heal *itself*. And so the vicious circle of self-perpetuating subsidy and substitution continues unabated.

It is at this critical point that 'natural' therapies (that is, measures that are in tune with nature) can helpfully intervene, both in the economic and health fields. (In the economic sphere, for example, smaller units and production processes can be set up in which the human being and not the machine is the guiding criterion, while growth in quality comes to count for more than mere increase in quantity. Compare E. F. Schumacher: *Small is Beautiful*.)

In the current manual, a number of major therapeutic approaches based on natural healing are offered as a means of self-help. To their number we now need to add the group of homoeopathic mineral salts or 'tissue-salts' discovered by Dr Wilhelm Heinrich Schüssler, after whom they are sometimes named. They are also sometimes referred to as 'cell salts' or 'biochemic remedies'.

Vital mineral salts The significance of the tissue-salts is explained on page 13 of Kurt Hickethier's *Lehrbuch der Biochemie*:

> A living cell uses up various substances. To the extent that the intake of vital substances is commensurate with their use, the cell remains healthy. If the various cells of the organism are healthy, the maintenance of harmony is assured. All the while the various organs of the human body are functioning smoothly, the person remains in a healthy state.
>
> The 'living substance' of the cell – that is, the cell fluid – contains all the substances that are necessary for it to survive, such as water, protein, fat, carbohydrates and salts. In comparison with the other components, the salts comprise only a minute proportion of the cell fluid ... yet 'the inorganic substances (salts) represented in the blood and tissues are sufficient to heal all illnesses that are capable of being healed at all'.

Dosage
It is not possible to offer exact details or generally applicable prescriptions here. Particularly where acute and/or serious health problems are concerned, it is advisable to seek advice from a healer or naturopathic doctor.

(Even the 'Biochemic Pharmacy' of the DHU – the

The twelve tissue-salts

No. Description	Usual abbreviation
Two calcium salts:	
1. Calcium fluoride (fluorspar)	Calc. Fluor.
2. Calcium phosphate (phosphate of lime)	Calc. Phos.
One sulphate:	
3. Calcium sulphate (gypsum)	Calc. Sulph.
One iron salt:	
4. Iron phosphate (phosphate of iron)	Ferr. Phos.
Three potassium salts:	
5. Potassium chloride (muriate of potash)	Kali Mur.
6. Potassium phosphate (phosphate of potash)	Kali Phos.
7. Potassium sulphate (sulphate of potash)	Kali Sulph.
One magnesium salt:	
8. Magnesium phosphate (phosphate of magnesium)	Mag. Phos.
Three sodium salts:	
9. Sodium chloride (common salt in molecular form)	Nat. Mur.
10. Sodium phosphate (phosphate of sodium)	Nat. Phos.
11. Sodium sulphate (sulphate of sodium)	Nat. Sulph.
One acid:	
12. Silicea (silicic acid or silicic oxide)	Silica

For nine of these twelve minerals* Schüssler recommends a homoeopathic potency of 6x. For *Calc. Fluor.*, *Ferr. Phos.* and *Silica*, however, he recommends 12x.

German Homoeopathic Association – which stocks these twelve remedies plus twelve further supplements, declines to give any prescribed dosage. Nor, in this book, shall we be going into the supplementary remedies or the ointments that are also available. This would exceed the book's remit, and would not make for clarity. It is, after all, the twelve tissue-salts that are the main, universal remedies.)

As a rule of thumb for dosage, however:
- suck 3 to 4 tablets two to three times a day;

*Translator's note: Available in the UK from chemists and health food shops, or from New Era Laboratories Ltd., Marfleet, Hull HU9 5NJ, generally in 6x potency. The British numbering shown above differs slightly from the German equivalent.

- for acute conditions, suck 1 tablet every 5 minutes to 1 hour;
- continue taking the tablets until the condition improves noticeably.

In a natural, healthy diet the tissue-salts or minerals are present in well-balanced proportions, and are easily absorbed and made use of.

These salts have a fortifying effect, and operate within the organism as living vehicles of synthesis and metabolism. (Sodium phosphate, for example, acts as a vehicle within the blood for taking away carbon dioxide.)

The *modus operandi* of the mineral salts

The Schüssler tissue-salts work by stimulating the body cells to produce those substances that are essential for the recovery and maintenance of health.

Thus, tissue-salt therapy makes no attempt to 'subsidize' or make good any health deficiency, or to provide stand-in substances that will sooner or later be used up or even (not infrequently) just not be absorbed at all, but merely excreted unused. Rather is their function to 'remind' the cells, and the organism as a whole, of their job of taking up and exploiting essential minerals. This ability is reduced, or even 'forgotten', as a result of such things as deficient diet, physical and psychosomatic illnesses and discordant psychic vibrations.

The twelve Schüssler remedies could be likened to instruction leaflets or programme notes. In homoeopathic form, these tissue-salts give our body cells the instructions or information they need to extract certain vital minerals from our food, and to apply them in the right way to the complex process that is our metabolism.

Homoeopathic dilution

It is their homoeopathic dilution that gives the remedies their great accessibility and reactivity. As a result of it, the tissue-salts are reduced to a size capable of passing through the cell membranes. It is for this reason that the Schüssler remedies are more effective in healing than minerals administered in non-homoeopathic form.

On this topic Hartwig Gabler writes in his *Wesen und Anwendung der Biochemie* that, among other things, they amount to 'targeted medical stimuli designed to

support or provoke the body's healing efforts in appropriate ways. For this purpose even the minutest quantities
of the substances concerned suffice, in the thinnest of
dilutions commensurate with their actual concentration
in the human blood and tissues.'

And again, 'The disturbed molecular flow that is typical of sick cells is smoothed out by mineral salt molecules
of similar type, with the result that the exchange of fluids
between the cell and the free extra-cellular tissues, formerly inhibited, is increased. The cell can then regenerate
biologically.'

These simplified descriptions of the cellular processes
will suffice to give us a generalized understanding of what
is involved.

It may be of interest to note that the 'instruction
leaflets' and 'programme notes' mentioned above can also
have an additional role to play in emergencies.

Stimulation versus substitution

Where a tissue-salt deficiency cannot be restored by
adopting a healthier diet – perhaps because the appropriate kind of food is no longer obtainable, or because the
regular supply is interrupted – an increased, longish-term
dosage of the relevant remedy can temporarily compensate
for the problem. In this case the remedy will be taking on
not merely a stimulatory function, but that of an actual
substitute.

By way of a simile, one could recall the fact that in
cases of severe fuel shortage it is always possible to burn
newspapers, instruction leaflets and programme notes on
the fire!

Exception: In cases of severe potassium deficiency it is
not sufficient to use the Schüssler salts as substitutes,
even though there are other types of mineral deficiency
that can be compensated for in this way. **It is absolutely
essential to have any suspected deficiency confirmed by a
competent healer and accorded expert treatment.**

**Combining the
twelve tissue-salts
with the healing
flower essences**

The following summary shows which tissue-salts are indicated by particular sets of symptoms, so that they can be
used to give homoeopathic support at the cellular level
to the use of healing flower essences in harmonizing
patients' personal vibrations.

Calc. Fluor.
(No. 1)

Summary of symptoms
Indicated, *inter alia*, for the treatment of
  torn ligaments;
  defects of the tooth enamel (sensitivity to heat and
    cold);
  over-production of hard skin (corns, calluses);
  hardening of the lymph nodes;
  brittle fingernails;
  varicose veins (painful inflammation of the veins);
  furring up of the arteries;
  coughing with porridgy expectoration;
  intense, burning pain when the 'elastic fibres' are over-
    stretched (displacement of the womb, sagging
    stomach muscles through overweight).

Calc. Fluor. is also an important component of the bone
surfaces, is vital in the mending of fractures, and promotes the development of a firm, elastic body in growing
children.

The first thing to do is to establish (as described above in
Chapter 1) which of the seven forms of vibrationary
disharmony is indicated, and then to select the corresponding essence or essences.

   If we then find that we have selected No. 25 (Red
Chestnut) or No. 26 (Rock Rose) from the **'Fear'** group as
appropriate to the case, or have found Nos. 14 (Heather)
or 18 (Impatiens) from the **'Loneliness'** group to be the
right one – and if one of the tell-tale symptoms listed
above is *also* apparent – then we can take it that *Calc.
Fluor.* belongs in the same vibrationary category.

   In such cases, then, the taking of *Calc. Fluor. 12x* is
recommended as a way of supplementing the use of
whichever one of the four listed healing flower essences is
chosen to promote the desired harmonization of the
psychic vibrations. In this way a parallel harmonization
can be encouraged at the cellular level.

   As with all aspects of self-help, though, an appropriate
measure of personal knowledge and intuition needs to be
balanced with an equal measure of responsibility for
seeking advice from a competent naturopath!

Complementary colour therapy
To go with *Red Chestnut* and *Rock Rose* from the 'Fear'
group, apply *yellow* at the acupuncture point CV 15.

To go with *Heather* and *Impatiens* from the 'Loneliness' group, irradiate the middle of the back with *green*.

Calc. Phos (No. 2) **Summary of symptoms**
Indicated, *inter alia*, as the main tissue-salt remedy for
bone weakness (Calc. Phos. is a prime constituent of
bone);
cramps, tingling, muscular numbness;
too high a pulse rate, plus associated sleeplessness
(that is, to quieten the heart), provided that the raised
pulse rate is not the result of 'blood dilution' and
resultant bloating of the tissues with water (in which
case see *Nat. Mur.*).

Calc. Phos. also contributes to blood production, as well
as acting as a binding agent for the organic formation of
protein within the system. Any deficiency of *Calc. Phos.*
in these areas is nevertheless not immediately apparent,
and is for a naturopath to diagnose.

The first task is to establish which of the seven vibrationary disharmonies is indicated, and then to select the
corresponding healing flower remedy.
If one has found No. 18 (Impatiens) from the '**Loneliness**' group to be appropriate and notices one of the
above symptoms, one can take it that *Calc. Phos.* belongs
to the same vibrationary category. In this case the administration of *Calc. Phos. 6x* is recommended in order
simultaneously to stimulate harmonization of the psychic
vibrations both at the cellular level and by means of the
healing flower essences.

Complementary colour therapy
Irradiate the middle of the back with *green*.

Calc. Sulph. **Summary of symptoms**
(No. 3*) *Calc. Sulph.* is *the* remedy for purulent conditions. It
encourages blood clotting, stimulates the metabolism and
strengthens the resistance. It is found in the liver and gall
bladder. It has an energizing effect and promotes detoxification, elimination and excretion.
Calc. Sulph. 6x should be taken for

*This salt is numbered 12 in the German system – Tr.

all inflammations that are simultaneously chronic and
    purulent, such as tonsillitis and bronchitis;
head colds with greenish yellow nasal discharge that
    contains blood and pus;
conjunctivitis and inflammations of the cornea;
inflammation of the middle ear;
inflammation of the urinary tract.

Such chronic, purulent inflammations either weaken the
immune system or are themselves brought about by a
weakening of the immune system, and always indicate
that the patient is seriously run down. It is vital in all such
cases to discover the source, such as a tooth with (unbe-
known to the patient) a rotting root.

Calc. Sulph. should also be used for dizziness last thing
at night (as a result of chronic, purulent inflammations),
for aggressive impulses towards anything and everything
– and particularly towards people who think differently
from oneself – as well as for chronic diarrhoea and a
craving for stimulants.

Calc. Sulph. corresponds to the resonances of five healing flower essences taken from two groups: from
the 'Fear' group Nos. 6 (Cherry Plum) and 25 (Red
Chestnut), and from the 'Uncertainty' group Nos. 12
(Gentian), 17 (Hornbeam) and 36 (Wild Oat).

Once it has been established which of the healing flowers
are appropriate, it will at once become apparent whether
they include any of the five just listed. In this event, **Calc.
Sulph. 6x** will be a suitable supplementary remedy for
promoting the healing process on the cellular level.

Complementary colour therapy
If the patient seems of an uncertain disposition and the
healing flower essences *Gentian, Hornbeam* or *Wild Oat*
have been chosen, *green* light should be applied to the
middle of the back, and *red* just below the breastbone.

If the patient tends towards the fearful or anxious –
that is, if the healing flower essences *Cherry Plum* and
Red Chestnut are applicable – *yellow* should be applied
to the acupuncture point CV 15.

Ferr. Phos.
(No. 4*)

Summary of symptoms
Ferr. Phos. is the main remedy for
    the early stages of inflammations, with resultant blood-
        congestion in the head and slight fever (in cases of

high fever, tissues are starting to die off, and attention should be paid to the digestion – see *Kali
Phos.*);
tired muscles;
pulsating, throbbing pains;
all throbbing sensations in unfamiliar places – with or
without pain (in the fingertips, teeth, ears or legs, for
example);
fresh wounds, cuts, bruises and sprains;
tiredness through lack of oxygen in the blood.

Ferr. Phos. attracts oxygen and thus serves as an oxygen
carrier: it is a vital mineral for maintaining the blood. All
the above symptoms demand an increased intake of *Ferr.
Phos.* so as to bring in more oxygen, a particular shortage
of which is directly indicated by the symptoms.

If the problems and pains listed above get worse with
movement and better with cold, this can be an important
aid to establishing that *Ferr. Phos.* is indicated.

Ferr. Phos. corresponds to the resonance-field of the
First Aid remedy, whether in drop or cream form. If it
is established that this special combination of healing
flower essences is a suitable aid to harmonization (see
page 19) *and* the symptoms listed above are in evidence at
the same time, *Ferr. Phos. 6x* can be a decisive factor in
activating the healing process.

Complementary colour therapy
At the onset of an inflammation or infection the middle of
the back should be irradiated with *green.*

The edges of the shoulder blades should also be irradiated with *red* to help raise the level of iron in the blood.
Caution! – irradiate for no longer than one minute at
most.

Kali Mur. **Summary of symptoms**
(No. 5) *Kali Mur.* is indicated for
acute inflammations, as a means of detoxification (for
the *early stages* of inflammations see *Ferr. Phos.*);
pleurisy, and a white to grey-white coated tongue (for a
yellow tongue coating see *Kali Sulph.*, and for a
yellowish-green one *Nat. Sulph.*);

*No. 3 according to the German system. The remaining salts then follow in
sequence – Tr.

coughing, with white or grey-white, stringy expectoration;

stringy mucus (from nose or genitals) that looks like
mealy powder when dry;

after unavoidable vaccinations;

thick, viscous, blackish blood.

From the resonance point of view, *Kali Mur.* corresponds to eight healing flower essences taken from the
groups 'Uncertainty', 'Over-sensitive' and 'Over-care'. If
one of the healing flower essences is chosen as suitable for
harmonizing the psychological frequencies *and* one of the
above symptoms is identified, *Kali Mur. 6x* can prove
effective in promoting the harmonization of the various
energies. (2 tablets of Kali Mur. 6x are often given every
half-hour until the condition changes.)

These eight healing flower essences are:

from the 'Uncertainty' group Nos. 12 (Gentian), 13
(Gorse), 28 (Scleranthus) and 36 (Wild Oat);

from the group entitled 'Over-sensitive to influences
and ideas' No. 33 (Walnut); and

from the group entitled 'Over-care for the welfare of
others' Nos. 3 (Beech), 8 (Chicory) and 32 (Vine).

Complementary colour therapy
If *Gentian, Gorse, Scleranthus* or *Wild Oat* are selected
as suitable healing flower essences from the 'Uncertainty'
group, or *Beech, Chicory* or *Vine* from the 'Overcare'
group, *green* should be applied to the middle of the back,
and *red* just below the breastbone.

In the case of *Walnut* from the 'Over-sensitive' group,
irradiate the nape of the neck with *blue*.

Kali Phos. (No. 6)   **Summary of symptoms**
Kali Phos. is the prime remedy for

high fever (above about 101.7°F or 38.8°C, in which
case 1 tablet of *Kali Phos. 6x* should be given every 3
minutes: the temperature will often come down from
106°F to around 99°F – or from 41°C to 38°C – in
as little as twenty minutes);

blood poisoning;

infected wounds;

sepsis of the mouth;

sticky, dirty-grey, smelly exudations of whatever kind.

Kali Phos. arrests tissue decay, and is regarded as *the* biochemic antiseptic.

Kali Phos. is also indicated by the following main symptoms:
  weakness or numbness of the nerves;
  muscular weakness and feelings of lameness;
  poor memory;
  nervousness;
  tearfulness;
  home-sickness;
  mistrust;
  worry and faint-heartedness;
  agoraphobia;
  ill-humours;
  nervous insomnia and sleepiness during the day.

If one or more of the symptoms listed is apparent, it may also be worth enlisting the services of an experienced specialist or dowser to determine whether the trouble may not be attributable to an underground watercourse beneath the sleeping quarters or workplace.

Kali Phos. corresponds to the resonance-fields of five essences from four different groups:
  from **'Uncertainty'** Nos. 13 (Gorse) and 17 (Hornbeam);
  from **'Not sufficient interest in present circumstances'** No. 23 (Olive);
  from **'Despondency or despair'** No. 22 (Oak);
  from **'Over-care for welfare of others'** No. 8 (Chicory).

If one of these five healing flower essences has been chosen as appropriate *and* one of the listed symptoms applies, *Kali Phos. 6x* promotes healing at those organic levels that correspond to the levels of psychic resonance stimulated by the flower essence.

Complementary colour therapy
To go with *Gorse* and *Hornbeam* from the 'Uncertainty' group and *Chicory* from the 'Over-care' group, irradiate the middle of the back with *green*, and also possibly the point just below the breastbone with *red*.

To go with *Olive* from the **'Not sufficient interest in present circumstances'** group, apply *turquoise* just beneath the breastbone and in the area of the throat.

To go with *Oak* from the **'Despondency or despair'** group, apply *orange* between the shoulder blades.

Kali Sulph.   **Summary of symptoms**
(No. 7)   *Kali Sulph.* is given in cases of
        slimy yellow secretions resulting from colds (catarrh, coughing, runny nose);
        slimy yellow tongue-coating;
        hangover;
        heaviness of head and limbs;
        dizziness and apathy;
        feelings of pressure and fullness in the stomach;
        scaling of the skin after illness (*Kali Sulph.* also assists new skin-growth)

Like *Ferr. Phos.*, *Kali Sulph.* is an oxygen carrier.

The need for *Kali Sulph.* is also indicated where the condition improves noticeably in the freshness of the open air and worsens in warmth and in the evening.

Kali Sulph. 6x is recommended for the recuperation stage following inflammations.

Kali Sulph. corresponds to the resonance-field of three healing flower essences from the group **'Not sufficient interest in present circumstances'** – namely Nos. 7 (Chestnut Bud), 16 (Honeysuckle) and 35 (White Chestnut).

If one of these remedies is identified as appropriate *and* one of the above symptoms is present, *Kali Sulph.* 6x can supply appropriate support on the physical level to the healing impulses supplied on the psychic level by the relevant healing flower remedy.

Complementary colour therapy
Apply *yellow* light just below the breastbone and *turquoise* to the throat area.

Mag. Phos.   **Summary of symptoms**
(No. 8)   *Mag. Phos.* is administered for
        all convulsive and spasmodic pains and complaints;
        gallstone colic (7 to 21 tablets of *Mag. Phos.* 6x to be dissolved in a glass of hot liquid and sipped slowly: in severe cases repeat until the spasms subside);
        labour pains (dosage as for gallstone colic above);
        sudden shooting, stabbing and/or boring pains (dosage as for gallstone colic above);

release of intestinal gases that brings no relief;

all glandular complaints (e.g. salivary, lymph or thyroid);

diseases of the liver and spleen;

pains that arise suddenly at intervals or with intermissions, and that are eased by pressure and warmth;

constipation;

dull pressure in the left-hand side of the abdomen due to inadequate activity of the spleen (normally diagnosable only by a practitioner);

any sleeplessness resulting from the above complaints.

Mag. Phos. is also responsible for the formation of sound, healthy bones in growing children and adolescents, as well as serving as an important remedy for the nerves – especially in the light of the current lack of magnesium in our diet.

Mag. Phos. corresponds to the resonance-field of two healing flower essences from the group **'Over-sensitive to influences and ideas'** – namely Nos. 4 (Centaury) and 15 (Holly).

If either of these is chosen *and* one of the symptoms mentioned is present, *Mag. Phos.* 6x can contribute materially on the organic level to the healing harmonization promoted on the psychic level by the corresponding healing flower remedy.

Complementary colour therapy

If the healing flower remedy *Holly* has been identified as appropriate, also irradiate with *orange* at the upper boundary of the pubic hair.

Nat. Mur. (No. 9)

Summary of symptoms

Nat. Mur. is common salt in homoeopathic dilution. It is responsible, with *Kali Phos.*, for the formation of new cells via the process of cell division.

It is administered for:

rheumatism in the joints;

noisy joints that crack and creak;

feelings of coldness in the hands, legs and back as a result of poor circulation (possible investigation by a naturopath is well worth considering);

shortage of stomach acid (signalled by, among other things, burning thirst, a burning throat or searing heartburn);

over-production of saliva or tears;
watery vomiting;
blisters with transparent, watery contents;
transparent, watery or glassy tongue-coating (or a
   clean tongue with bubbles of saliva at its edges);
loss of taste and smell;
coughing with frothy expectoration;
toothache extending to half the face;
trigeminal or facial neuralgia (*tic-douloureux*);
caries (cavities in the teeth);
scaling of the scalp.

In whatever form, common salt attracts water. In the absence of the proper form of salt, the body would dry out – a process whose early stages are often characterized by constipation.

Intolerance of stuffy air in damp homes, and a tendency to feel better in dry, clean air are likewise symptoms indicating *Nat. mur.*

Nat. Mur. corresponds to the resonance-fields of three healing essences from the group '**Despondency or despair**' – namely Nos. 10 (Crab Apple), 11 (Elm) and 29 (Star of Bethlehem).

If one of these three healing flower essences has been recognized as potentially helpful for the harmonizing of the psychic vibrations *and* one of the symptoms just described is present, *Nat. Mur. 6x* can add significant impetus to the healing process.

Complementary colour therapy
Irradiate the area between the shoulder blades with *orange*.

If the healing flower remedy *Crab Apple* is indicated as suitable, apply additional irradiation with *violet* to the middle of the upper boundary of the pubic hair and on top of the crown of the head (the so-called 'crown chakra').

Nat. Phos.
(No. 10)

Summary of symptoms
Nat. Phos. is used in natural healing for
   raised uric acid levels and over-acidity of the blood
      (this needs to be checked by a practitioner) – both
      often being the result of excessive sugar intake and
      protein consumption;
   creamy, honey-like exudations;

reducing pus formation (from wounds, unclean skin or
purulent inflammations of the body, for example);
acid belching or 'heartburn' as a result of over-acidity
(not to be confused with the 'searing heartburn'
listed as a symptom under *Nat. Mur.* above);
acid vomiting of 'cheesy' material;
diarrhoea containing apparently 'minced' material of a
yellowish green colour.

Nat. Phos. corresponds to the resonance-field of two
healing flower essences from the group 'Not sufficient
interest in present circumstances' – namely Nos. 21
(Mustard) and 37 (Wild Rose).

If either of these essences is pinpointed as being suitable
and one of the above symptoms is noticed, *Nat. Phos. 6x*
can stimulate the healing process on those physical levels
at which healing is also stimulated, in terms of psychic
resonance, by the corresponding healing flower essence.

Complementary colour therapy
Apply *yellow* just below the breastbone, and *turquoise* to
the throat area.

Nat. Sulph.
(No. 11)

Summary of symptoms
Nat. Sulph. helps to eliminate surplus waste products
from the cells, and is involved in the work of the liver. It is
used in cases of
the vomiting of bile and/or bilious diarrhoea;
inadequate supply of bile to the colon and consequent
digestive disorders involving constipation with cutting internal pains;
jaundice (resulting from bile in the blood!);
weak metabolism;
heaviness and weakness in the calves;
light-headedness;
coughing with greenish expectoration that is difficult
to dislodge.
The symptoms worsen in warm, damp conditions and
stuffy air (that is, a so-called 'hot-house climate').

Nat. Sulph. corresponds to the resonance-fields of five
healing essences:
from the 'Fear' groups, Nos. 2 (Aspen) and 20
(Mimulus), and from the 'Despondency or despair'
group, Nos. 11 (Elm), 19 (Larch) and 24 (Pine).

After choosing the appropriate healing flower essences the thing to do is once again to establish whether one of the five listed is among them *and* whether one of the above symptoms is also present. Where this is the case, *Nat. Sulph. 6x* will provide the appropriate complementary treatment on the organic level to the harmonization of the psychic vibrations afforded by the relevant healing essence.

Complementary colour therapy

If the patient needs the healing flower essences *Aspen* or *Mimulus* from the 'Fear' group, acupuncture point CV 15 should be irradiated with *yellow*.

If the patient needs *Elm, Larch* or *Pine* from the **'Despondency or despair'** group, *orange* is applied between the shoulder blades.

Silica (No. 12)   ### Summary of symptoms

Silica – also known as Silicea, silicic acid or silicic oxide – lends firmness, elasticity, resilience and life to the connective tissue. Any lack of *Silica* leads to premature ageing. In naturopathy it is administered for

> jangling, over-sensitive nerves;
> jumpiness;
> distraughtness;
> hair loss (for scaling of the scalp see *Nat. Mur.*);
> bleeding;
> rheumatic complaints (*Silica* absorbs uric acid);
> sweaty feet;
> disturbed and unrefreshing sleep;
> involuntary jerking of the arms and legs while half-asleep;
> headache above the eyes;
> pains in the temples;
> sciatica, and pain in the hips and the small of back;
> constipation as a result of temporarily reduced intestinal activity.

In addition, *Silica* helps to prevent furring-up of the arteries and assists with the elimination of pus.

Silica belongs to the resonance-fields of two essences from the **'Uncertainty'** group – namely Nos. 17 (Hornbeam) and 36 (Wild Oat).

If one of these healing flower essences is recognized as

appropriate *and* one of the symptoms mentioned is simultaneously present, *Silica 12x* can supply material support on the cellular level for the harmonization of the psychic vibrations afforded by the relevant essence.

Complementary colour therapy
Irradiate the middle of the back with *green*, and apply *red* just underneath the breastbone.

The reader will meanwhile have noticed that not all the thirty-eight healing flower essences have been allocated to one or the other of the twelve Schüssler remedies or tissue-salts. This is due to the fact that not all of the thirty-eight healing flowers have resonances that exactly complement those of the twelve Schüssler salts.

This is not of course to say that those not listed are any less health-giving or harmonious, but merely that they do not stand in the same complementary relationship to specific tissue-salts as those actually mentioned.

Finally, an important note regarding the therapeutic supplementation of healing flower essences with tissue-salts:

We are unable either to confirm or to recommend other systems of allocation based not on everyday healing practice, but on astrological or esoteric considerations – or even pure whim.

5. Kirlian photography: life-energy made visible

An illustrated introduction Kirlian photography is a pioneering method of rapid diagnosis that has already proved its practical worth to those healers who know how to handle it.

At this point, therefore, we propose to take a look at this diagnostic technique, even though it is not of immediate concern to self-help therapy. It does, after all, reflect directly on the notion that 'the right vibration heals'.

The human organism as energy-generator and vibrational field In Kirlian photography patterns of discharge, or radiation, from the hands or feet are captured optically by recording them directly on photographic paper. The images appear when, using special apparatus, a particular (quite harmless) high frequency field is generated beneath the paper.

Results of Kirlian photography

With the aid of Kirlian photography it becomes optically apparent, and thus tangibly demonstrable

that every human being is an energy-generator or vibrational field;

that a person's state of energy or vibration determines his or her mental, psychological and physical condition and that, conversely, mind, psyche and *soma* determine the strength and nature of the relevant energies and vibrations (there is, in other words, a constant, reciprocal interplay of effects);

that, thanks to Kirlian photography, and to the fact that the various characteristic energy and vibration patterns can thus be seen for the first time, the existence of these energies and vibrations can now be proved;

that, in consequence, we have a unique opportunity to observe *changes* in such patterns, to compare vibrational states as they are revealed by Kirlian photography, and to draw *conclusions* from them about a person's health and state of mind;

that Kirlian photography offers us the chance to establish in a matter of minutes what a person's energy state is *before* and *after* treatment with a given homoeopathic remedy, with one of the healing flower essences or with colour therapy, for example, and to observe just how the organism reacts to it.

It was the Soviet couple Semyon and Valentina Kirlian who first developed this unique technique, initially dubbing it 'electrophotography within a high frequency field'.

In the interim, Kirlian photography has been elaborated world-wide for purposes of research and diagnosis. In the process, a variety of practical procedures have been worked out, as well as a range of somewhat differing interpretations of the phenomena observed.

Auric images

A good many researchers start from the assumption that a Kirlian photograph represents the vibrational pattern of the *aura*. Others insist that it represents a picture of the soul. Yet others see Kirlian images merely as patterns of electrical discharge revealing no more than the current state of the subject's skin conductivity.

Often the energy depicted is called 'bio-plasma' or 'bio-energy'. Other researchers speak of 'bio-photons' or 'bio-electric vibration'. Yet others attribute the energy patterns to the so-called *od*, or *prana*.

What is certain, however, is that

- in some branches of American psychiatry Kirlian photography is used to make a quick diagnosis of the energy-state of otherwise unresponsive patients.
- in Britain the Kirlian technique is used to unearth clues to psychological blockages.
- in German-speaking parts of Europe and other neighbouring countries it is used in daily practice by healers and naturopaths, as well as by open-minded, progressive dentists and hospital doctors.

Photographic techniques
A variety of photographic techniques are used.

Many users prefer black-and-white pictures, while others prefer colour prints. Whereas in the West Kirlian photos are mainly taken of the hands or feet, or even merely of the fingertips, in Romania experiments have been done involving whole body Kirlian photography.

In Germany the valuable and authoritative pioneering work of Peter Mandel deserves special mention. A committed researcher and experienced healer, as well as a seminar leader and writer of specialist books on the subject, he has acquired a formidable reputation in the sphere of Kirlian photography and colour therapy.

Diagnostic criteria
Among the diagnostic points to watch for are:
  the presence or absence of radiating fibres or 'coronas';
  whether any given corona is whole or broken;
  whether the corona is tightly-packed, 'glutinous' or uneven;
  and whether the corona is even all the way round.

This last indicates free flowing energies and an optimal state of health.

Optical proof of the effectiveness of natural remedies

The Kirlian 'before and after' pictures of hands and feet reproduced on page 113 show that:
  Kirlian photography permits conclusions to be drawn about the patient's state of energy;
  healing flower essences or colour therapy and homoeopathy produce immediate changes in the energy picture;
  the true causes of energy blockages often become visible on the photo only *after* dosage or treatment.
  specific indications are frequently to be found regarding particular problem areas, such as the kidneys, the effects of dental amalgam and so on.

The captions beneath the pictures are intended only for illustration, and have deliberately been kept brief.

42-year-old woman teacher

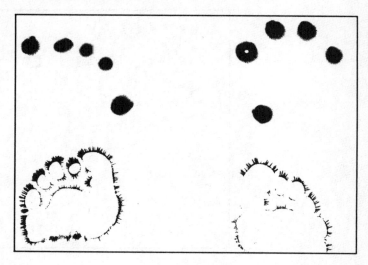

Before
Symptoms: psychological problems arising from marital separation, plus deficient metabolism

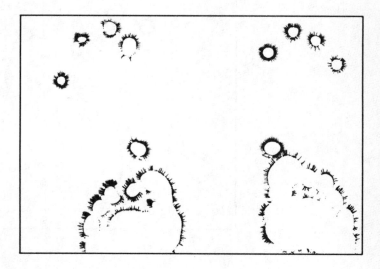

After
Following colour irradiation and administration of the healing flower essences Mimulus, Clematis, Heather and White Chestnut

27-year-old male actor

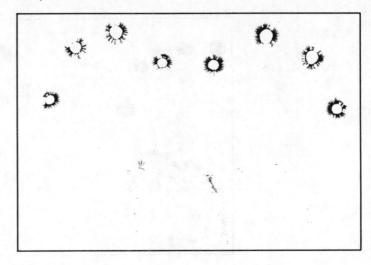

Before
Symptoms: weak nerves, cramps in the right arm

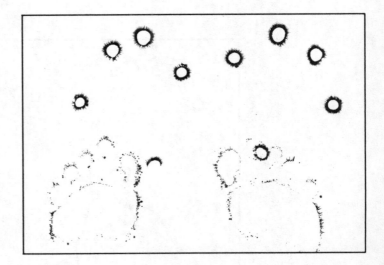

After
Following administration of the healing flower essences Crab Apple, Chestnut Bud, Sweet Chestnut and Water Violet, and removal of all traces of dental amalgam from the system by means of homoeopathic detoxification (Merc. sol., Cupr., Stann.)

49-year-old businesswoman

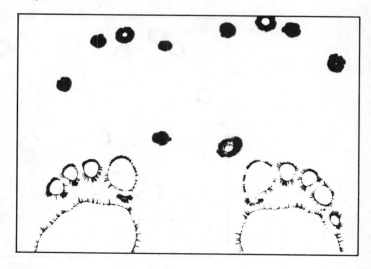

Before
Symptoms: stiffness of the fingers with pain; deficient metabolism

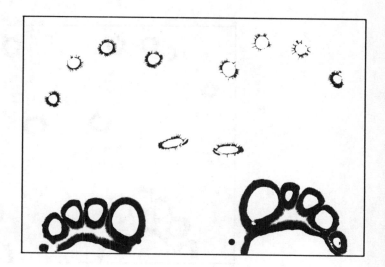

13 days after
Following homoeopathic detoxification of the cortisone in the body, three irradiations of the liver points with yellow light and administration of the healing essences Centaury, Crab Apple, Mustard, Star of Bethlehem and White Chestnut

39-year-old female secretary

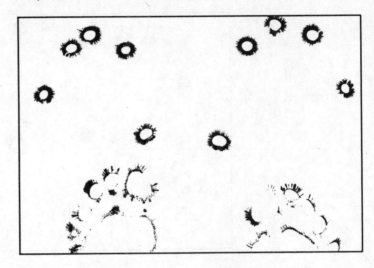

Before
Symptoms: disturbed sleep

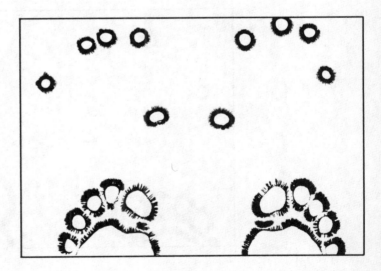

After
Following administration of the healing flower essences Impatiens, Pine, Red Chestnut, Rock Water, Wild Rose and a single session of colour therapy

Naturally the pictures and brief comments above do not attempt to give a comprehensive description of the complex findings, diagnostic procedures or therapeutic techniques involved. Rather are they just a few examples of how Kirlian photography can help us understand, interpret and treat the human being as a vehicle and generator of energy-vibrations and as a unitary energy-field.

Film diagnosis as an early-warning aid

Kirlian diagnosis offers a quicker and simpler route to clinical diagnosis. Quite often a Kirlian picture shows the *initial* stages of an illness, before any symptoms become clinically apparent.

It is to be hoped that this fascinating technique will be further researched, developed and put to good use for humanity's benefit.

6. Colour meditations and affirmations to accompany the healing flower essences

An introduction to meditation as a healing frequency

Meditation is the profound and comprehensive relaxation of body, mind, intellect and soul, in such a way as to permit one to let go of all cares, sorrows, confused thoughts, negative feelings and anxieties.

During this time of letting go the primal harmony of the soul or self is revealed – in the form of tranquillity, joy, peace, love, light or other sensations and perceptions.

Meditation can also entail a conscious striving for higher levels of mental, ethical and spiritual development.

However one sees it, this time of quiet – this respite from the drudgery of daily life lasting for a few minutes, a quarter of an hour, perhaps even half an hour – serves to regenerate body, mind and soul. In the course of meditation most people sense within them the opening up of new dimensions of consciousness that offer fresh insights into the challenges and problems facing them. They are also aware through meditation of an inflow of unsuspected new energies 'topping up their inner batteries'.

Creative stillness

Paradoxical though it may seem, the apparent emptiness of non-action, the supposed void of a stilled mind, can bring about a reconnection with the primal creative powers that are at work within every human being and without which life itself cannot exist. (This vital reconnection with the primal creative force is also universally re-established during deep sleep, when it equally serves to 'recharge our life batteries'.)

For millennia those who have been accustomed to turn within in this way have known that meditation can also bring about healing. Not that meditation is any guarantee of a miracle cure. But it *is* of great help in harmonizing the psychic vibrations and opening up the energies of spiritual awareness. In this way meditation contributes to people's overall recovery and healing – in body, mind and soul – and thus also promotes the various individual healing processes. At which point the link with our theme 'the right vibration heals' is once again established.

Measurable effects Modern technology has made it possible to measure the changes brought about by meditation within the body, and particularly within the brain.

Among other findings (since published), it has been established that during relaxed meditation

the circulation becomes more stable;

the metabolism is affected positively;

the breath is freed to flow naturally, without being distorted by thoughts or irregularities imposed by the conscious mind;

the more tranquil, more harmonious state of mind involved has psychosomatic effects on the meditator's entire condition;

whereas in normal life the brainwaves reveal a constant, discordant succession of excitements and tensions, in meditation they become converted to relaxed, harmonic frequencies that are decisive in promoting positive living and creative action.

We therefore propose to the reader a series of harmonizing and healing meditation aids that are quite simple and easy to apply.

In these recommendations for meditation the various *colour-frequencies* are used to supplement the seven main groups of healing flower essences, while the *affirmations* (designed to strengthen the power of positive thinking) are used to supplement the thirty-eight individual remedies that Edward Bach personally allocated to the relevant states of mind.

Meditation guide (A summary will be found on page 122.)

Introductory remarks **Duration**
To begin with, meditate for 5 to 10 minutes only, later for perhaps 20 to 30 minutes, or possibly longer under expert guidance. What matters is the quality – the degree of real tranquillity and relaxation attained – not the quantity.

Surroundings
Switch off the radio, television, computer or whatever. Seek out some quiet spot for yourself that is neither too hot nor too cold – perhaps even your own special room. Just for this brief time, too, disconnect the telephone so that its ringing cannot disturb you.

Time
You can happily meditate at whatever times suit you. As a general rule, though, you are recommended to set aside a fixed time for meditation, and in particular the early morning and evening.

Posture
For the average European the most suitable posture for meditating is sitting upright in a comfortable position. Some would rather lie down, but this can quite easily result in falling asleep. Certain seated Yoga postures are helpful for maintaining alert awareness, provided that they can be maintained without discomfort – but these are certainly not essential.

Typical experiences during meditation
Often tiredness will be experienced at the beginning of a meditation, either because one is genuinely worn out or because the system has not yet adjusted to the quieter vibrational regime experienced during meditation. Tiredness is a problem that can easily be overcome simply by staying alert and attentive to the content of the meditation.

Nearly all meditators also 'see' a variety of images, lights, colours and so on, or sense various subtle energies. This is quite normal and natural. Phenomena of this kind represent transitional stages as the consciousness begins to reconnect with its primal, creative source.

Motivation
The best guarantee that a meditation will 'succeed' is one's own personal motivation. Provided that one aligns oneself with positive ends and applies positive means, both the course of the meditation and its results will also be positive.

General guide to all the colour meditations with their relevant affirmations

1. Sit comfortably and erect, and avoid all possible disturbances for the short time involved.
2. Establish which of the healing flower essences is most appropriate to your current state of vibration, noting that:

    for the purposes of each meditation, only *one* flower essence should be settled on; and that

    the appropriate flower can be identified in a variety of ways – intuitively (using the Healing Flower Color Cards, see page 127) or by reading the descriptions listed on pages 11 onwards.
3. Read the corresponding affirmation and commit it to memory (see pages 123 ff, or the cards themselves*). Then, on the basis of the colour summary (once again see either pages 123 ff or the cards themselves) decide which of the meditation colours listed you are immediately drawn towards.
4. Then close your eyes and breathe in deeply three times through your nose, so that not only your lungs, but also your diaphragm and midriff (in other words, your whole abdomen) are filled with air – as it were to the very tips of your toes: each time breathe out just as deeply, but through your mouth.
5. Now turn all your attention to the affirmation and let it run through your mind (some even find it helpful to say the affirmation aloud in a low voice). The aim is to 'concentrate' on it – to focus both your thoughts and your feelings on this single affirmation and to submerge yourself in the power of its vibrations. Observe the extent to which your general attitude changes.
6. After a little while (say 3 to 5 minutes) shift your awareness away from the affirmation and instead visualize the colour that you have already chosen in advance. Visualize it streaming into your body from above via the top of your head (the so-called crown centre), in the form of a clear, benign light, and spreading from there into your whole body. Many people associate the inflow of the coloured light with the in-breath and the sense of well-being as it spreads within the body with the outbreath. It is a matter of personal preference, though, whether one lets the coloured light that is flooding through one flow out again

*Where book and cards differ slightly in wording, either will of course do. – Tr.

through the body and out via the feet,

via the upper abdomen between the navel and the ribcage (the so-called solar plexus centre),

via the chest (the so-called heart centre),

or in a purely generalized sense by way of the whole body.

7. Carry on this exercise of imagining coloured light streaming into you from above for just a few minutes or for as long as seems agreeable. Be consciously aware of the coloured light vibrating within you.

8. Bring your brief meditation to a close again by re-aligning yourself mentally or intuitively with your affirmation. Notice how far your understanding of the affirmation has changed, perhaps even deepened. Also make a note of whether you are now feeling different, and possibly better than before.

9. Conclude the exercise by breathing deeply in and out once more.

The exercise again, in abbreviated, easily memorized form:

1. Sit in a relaxed, upright position.
2. Choose – whether by looking it up or otherwise – your affirmation and colour.
3. Commit the affirmation to memory.
4. Close your eyes, breathe in deeply through your nose and out deeply through your mouth.
5. Concentrate your thoughts on the affirmation.
6. Imagine the coloured light flowing into you from above and flowing out again via the feet, abdomen, heart or simply the whole body.
7. Sense the vibration of the coloured light within you.
8. Return your concentration to the affirmation, and observe the sensations and effects brought about by the exercise.
9. Bring the meditation to a close by breathing in and out more deeply.

38 affirmations for the 38 healing flower essences and special meditation colours for the seven healing flower groups

Affirmations

For each flower essence an affirmation is given that expresses in positive form those points that Edward Bach, in allocating his thirty-eight remedies plus the First Aid remedy identified as being disharmonious or problematical, and thus as presenting specific goals to be striven for.

The affirmations thus embody in condensed, concise

form precisely those positive mental energies that are capable of harmonizing the particular, disturbed states of mind that he described.

Thoughts, words and feelings are known to represent powerful energies. Affirmations make use of these forces to produce positive fields of vibration.

Colours

For each of the seven main groups of healing flower essences three (sometimes four) special colours are proposed for colour-meditation.

These meditation-colours offer subtle help in healing and in reinforcing the vibrations of the particular healing flower essences that relate to the seven main groups of mind-states.

Each of these colours admittedly corresponds – seen from one particular level, at least – to a vibration that may be predominantly physical, mental or spiritual in nature. But this should not affect your choice of colour, which should be made intuitively – with the help of the special colour cards, for example (see pages 127–30).

Even imaginary colours can be sensed directly and experienced subjectively. For this reason the colour-meditations have amply proved their worth, in line with the motto 'The right vibration heals'.

(Some readers will also wish to experiment within the context of ordinary colour therapy with the meditation colours that follow: see also the details of hand-held colour lamps on pages 132–3.)

Group 1: 'Fear' ## Meditation colours
Violet (physical), **blue** (mental), **white or gold** (spiritual).

Affirmations
Rock Rose (26): 'God loves me and gives me confidence. I am filled with new hope.'
Mimulus (20): 'I can let go of everything that burdens me from the past. I have new courage.'
Cherry Plum (6): 'Within me is an inner source from which I can draw strength to fulfil whatever I need to do.'
Aspen (2): 'I can face the future with confidence. I am being guided.'
Red Chestnut (25): 'Everybody's life-plan is different. Each leads to perfection in its own way.'

Group 2: 'Uncertainty'	**Meditation colours**
	Turquoise (physical), **blue** (mental), **gold-green** (spiritual)

Affirmations

Cerato (5): 'I accept responsibility for my own life. I trust my inner voice.'

Scleranthus (28): 'I invoke inner balance and clarity. My decisions are sure.'

Gentian (12): 'I can cope with all my problems. I have the courage to grow in my own good time, just as nature does.'

Gorse (13): 'Life is a gift. I respect and use it as such.'

Hornbeam (17): 'I have a life-task to perform. The creative force helps me to fulfil it.'

Wild Oat (36): 'I open myself to my intuitive impulses. I trust my soul.'

Group 3: 'Not sufficient interest in present circumstances'

Meditation colours

Green (physical), **gold** (mental), **gold or white** (spiritual)

Affirmations

Clematis (9): 'I observe my thoughts. I decide consciously which of them are in my own best interests, and act accordingly.'

Honeysuckle (16): 'I treasure all my pleasant memories. Every day I consciously try to bring joy to others.'

Wild Rose (37): 'The creative power has given me the chance to be free. I am using this freedom to lead a beautiful and creative life.'

Olive (23): 'I am entitled to let go and enjoy myself. In this way I let new energies flood through me.'

White Chestnut (35): 'Within me is peace. Its harmony gives me inner and outer balance.'

Mustard (21): 'Cheerful, bright light helps me to feel harmony and joy and to radiate them to others.'

Chestnut Bud (7): 'I recognize my faults and behaviour patterns, and am prepared to learn from them.'

Group 4: 'Loneliness'

Meditation colours

Green (physical), **turquoise** (mental), **pink** (spiritual).

Affirmations

Water Violet (34): 'Life is a matter of giving and taking. I can both give support and love, and accept them too.'

Impatiens (18): 'Everything has its time. I calmly open myself up to mine.'

Heather (14): 'My best friend is my own soul. I am at one with it.'

Group 5: 'Over-sensitive to influences and ideas'

Meditation colours

Pink (physical), **violet** (mental), **white or gold** (spiritual).

Affirmations

Agrimony (1): 'All development demands stability. I am both loving and firm at once.'

Centaury (4): 'My life-task deserves my recognition and conscious devotion.'

Walnut (33): 'I am prepared both to enter into a give-and-take with others and to stick to my own path.'

Holly (15): 'Life gives to all of us what is ours. I open myself to what is mine.'

Group 6: 'Despondency or despair'

Meditation colours

Pink (physical), **gold-green** (mental), **white** (spiritual).

Affirmations

Larch (19): 'God loves me and wants me to be everything that I can be with the aid of His grace and my own efforts.'

Pine (24): 'Good as I am at identifying my faults, I am learning to rejoice even in my imperfections.'

Elm (11): 'I listen to my inner call and follow it.'

Sweet Chestnut (3): 'I can let go and let the creative power bear me up.'

Star of Bethlehem (29): 'My soul finds consolation in the divine light.'

Willow (38): 'I am drawing new strength to myself so as to lead a happier and more aware life.'

Oak (22): 'I feel strength within me, and at the same time a calm serenity.'

Crab Apple (10): 'I am breathing out everything that is dark, burdensome and unclean. I am breathing in serenity, purity and confidence.'

Group 7: 'Over-care for the welfare of others'

Meditation colours

Turquoise (physical), **white** (mental), **gold** (spiritual).

Affirmations

Chicory (8): 'I am able to love myself. I recognize that we each have to develop according to our own individual life-plan.'

Vervain (31): 'All kinds of energies are flowing within me. I hold myself open to any new impulses that life may bring.'

Vine (32): 'I am learning to distinguish between when to let go and when to hang on.'

Beech (3): 'We are each responsible for our own life. I am learning to realize what my own responsibility is.'

Rock Water (27): 'Life's colourful diversity is the expression of creative joy. I am allowing this creative joy to flood through me.'

First Aid remedy   **Meditation colours**
Violet (physical), **white** (mental), **gold** (spiritual).

Affirmation
'I ask for help and divine guidance.'

7. The healing flower color cards

A totally new approach to selecting the right healing flowers and colours In this handbook we offer (for the first time) a very simple do-it-yourself method for selecting directly the particular flower remedies and healing colours that apply to you personally – namely the Healing Flower Color Cards.

The use of these cards and the principle underlying them are soon explained ...

The complete pack

The complete pack of colour cards consists of:

1. 38 cards with,

   on the front,

   – pictures of the healing flowers by the Austrian artist Silvia Reili-Preinfalk, which are particularly effective at expressing the particular resonance of each flower.

   – the designation of the group to which the flower belongs according to Edward Bach,

   – its name, plus its standard international reference number, and

   – a brief indication of its main or most frequent application, plus,

   on the back,

   – the corresponding colour, as per the assignment of colour-therapies to healing flowers in Chapter two of this book.

2. 39 cards with,

   on the front,

   – pictures of the thirty-eight healing flowers plus the composite First Aid remedy,

   – the name and reference number, plus the relevant affirmation as listed and explained in Chapter six above;

and on the back,
  – the three meditation colours appropriate for medi-
    tating on the spiritual, mental and physical levels.

Thus, the complete pack contains two sets of cards total-
ling seventy-seven in all, together with a detailed guide.
These Swiss-made 'Healing Flower Color Cards' © by
AGM were formerly sold under the name 'Bach Flower
Color Cards', and are available from all good bookshops.
In North America they can be obtained from US Games.

The idea behind the thirty-eight Healing Flower Color Cards ©:

Lay people often have difficulty in deciding with any
speed or certainty whether the description of a particular
psychological or emotional state applies to them personally. Either they find that a *whole range* of definitions fits,
and are therefore unable to settle on only one or two, or
possibly they do not recognize themselves as described at
all.
  Healers, too, often find that patients are unable to
express themselves clearly enough, and feel that it is high
time that some quick, uncomplicated initial diagnostic
tool was available.

Intuition to the rescue

The Healing Flower Color Cards come as something of
a godsend, therefore. They permit direct, intuitive access
to, and immediate realization of, the healing factor that is
the very subject of this book – namely the 'right vibration'.
  Not only the fronts of the cards, with their sensitive
representations of all the healing flowers, but also the
backs of the cards, with their bright healing colours, offer
us the opportunity to feel directly drawn to this card or
that – a process in which unconscious impulses will naturally also have a role to play. To this extent the Healing
Flower Color Cards may be compared with the Tarot
pack. The principle underlying them is that of the con-
currence, at any one moment, between the patient's mental and emotional attitudes towards a given problem,
question or topic, and the resulting choice of one or more
cards at *that particular moment in time*. The depth-
psychologist C. G. Jung called the principle underlying
this kind of sensory coincidence 'synchronicity'.

The pack of cards

There now follow instructions for using the 38 color cards.

A. Determining the appropriate flowers by means of the colours

Simply by choosing a colour, and then a single card, you can find your way intuitively to the particular healing flowers that suit you.

1. Collect yourself for a few seconds, and think of your state of health as you would *like* it to be.
2. Then shuffle the cards and lay them down before you in a semicircular fan on any flat surface, with their coloured backs uppermost.
3. Let yourself be guided to whichever card seems to you to symbolize your optimum state of physical health, and take that card.
4. Then let yourself be guided to whichever card seems to stand for your optimum state of *mental* health, and take that card too.
5. Read the descriptions and brief summaries printed on each; if you like, look up the more detailed notes in Chapter 1 above, too.
6. Take both of the healing flower essences indicated, in the familiar dilution of about 4 drops to one glass of water. Also consult Chapter 2, to see which colour therapy procedure may also be relevant.

B. Determining the appropriate healing flowers and/or healing colours with the aid of the flower pictures

Intuitive selection

You can also make your selection intuitively on the basis of the particular 'vibes' that you get from the illustrations themselves.

1. Once again start by collecting yourself, and 'tune in' to your idea of your optimum state of health.
2. Now shuffle the cards and lay them down next to one another in overlapping rows, in such a way that the pictures can be seen, but *not* the names, group and so on.
3. Then let yourself be guided by turns – and as far as possible, purely on the basis of your momentary preference – to the two cards that strike you as being most propitious for your bodily health and mental harmony respectively.
4. Take these two cards, read what is printed beneath the pictures, look at the colours on the back, and take the corresponding healing flower essences in

the usual dilution, or apply the corresponding colours as described in Chapter 2.

Meanwhile one particular point is applicable to both methods. Experience has shown that not too many essences should be taken at once. For this reason we recommend that two – or at most three or four – essences be regarded as the limit, to start with at least.

In this way the Healing Flower Color Cards © *bring together in card form vital information on the healing vibrations of the flowers, brief details of groups, names, number and primary uses, and the healing colour-frequencies themselves. Both healers and lay people can use them without difficulty.*

The Healing Flower Color Cards © *are also out-standingly suited to the selection of healing flowers and healing colours by intuitive healers and lay people alike, in conjunction with any other book on the healing flowers.*

Conclusion

Health is more a psychic frequency than a physically measurable bodily condition to be pursued by purely orthodox medical means.

Health, wholeness (the word is related to 'holiness'), and holism are the very essence and nature of our soul. All of us live from – and in – a single, creative energy field, whether we call it 'God' (as many do) or something else.

Our life can be for us a process of self-perfection leading to a conscious merging with this primal energy. Humanity's great teachers such as Lao Tse, the Buddha, Jesus Christ, Master Eckhart, Saint-Germain, Samuel Hahnemann, Ramana Maharshi, Sant Darshan Singh and not least Edward Bach have not only realized this insight, but constantly remind us of it. They were and are ready to help us.

'Illness' has a special role to play in our lives. Once there is no longer anything to remind us of the soul's origin and goal, once we have finally abandoned the harmony of creation, we use illnesses (self-caused and self-created) to set ourselves specific tasks that we can then no longer ignore, and whose function is to force us consciously to rediscover that primal state of harmony.

With the right vibration – with divine, psychic and earthly energies finally brought into harmony – we can lead more fruitful lives, filled with less suffering and more love!

Colour therapy and colour meditation using a handheld colour therapy and colour acupuncture lamp

Life Energy Products Santa Fe offers a *MultiColor Combi*® Set (available in Europe) that is ideal for colour therapy, colour acupuncture, colour meditation, chakra activation and colour experimentation. It consists of a powerful portable lamp, two sets of fifteen selected colour-filters made of special film, a special attachment containing a pyramid of quartz glass and other accessories.

The main colours used in colour therapy – yellow, orange, red, pink, light green, green, turquoise, blue, violet and purple/magenta – are among the basic colours provided, together with a variety of other shades.

All the colour-filters can be used either individually or in combination, thus permitting the production of any particular shade desired.

The quartz glass pyramid can be placed at any distance for colour acupuncture, for colour meditation and to intensify the vibrations of the various colours.

A detailed booklet is included giving precise instructions for use. This covers topics such as the harmonization of personal vibrations, normalization of body-fluid regimes, use in cases of nervousness, feelings of weakness, psychological problems and recurrent complaints such as nasal blockage and digestive problems, as well as for meditation and awakening the chakras.

All the applications of colour described in this book can be carried out with the aid of this handheld colour-lamp.

Thus, this easy-to-use colour set offers a variety of possible uses not only to the experienced healer, but also to ordinary people who would like to treat themselves or to experiment with colours. The European suppliers of the lamp are WRAGE Versandservice, whose address is Schlüterstraße 4, D-2000 Hamburg 13, Germany (tel. 040/455240). Readers in the United States who are interested in obtaining the lamp should contact Life Energy Products, whose address is 1310 Cibola Circle, Santa Fe, New Mexico 87501 (fax. 505 986 0235).

Seminars with the authors

Ingrid von Rohr is available for seminars in English or German. She teaches Natural Complementary Medicine for medical professionals and for lay people. Wulfing von Rohr holds meditation seminars.

For German language seminars in Switzerland, Germany and Austria please contact Integra Seminare, P.O. Box 7447, CH 6000 Luzern 7, Switzerland (phone 01041/41/229860, fax 01041/41/227184).

For seminars in the UK and in North America Ingrid is ready to accept invitations by seminar organizations or ad hoc groups of interested individuals, which should be directed to NKM Academy, 1310 Cibola Circle, Santa Fe, NM 87501, USA (for North American enquiries) or to NKM Akademie, Waldweg 8, D 80022 Grünwald b. München, Germany (for European enquiries).

Bibliography

General reading

Aurobindo, Sri, *Synthesis of Yoga*, Aurobindo Ashram, 1990.

Blavatsky, H. P., *Isis Unveiled*, Theosophical Publishing House, USA, 1972.

Griscom, C., *The Healing of Emotion*, Bantam, 1990.

Griscom, C., *Time is an Illusion*, Bantam, 1989.

Harf, A. and Rohr, W. von, *Yoga – Weg zur Harmonie*, Falken, 1989.

Kraaz, I. S. von Rohr, *Die neue Weiblichkeit*, 1991, Kösel, Munich.

Rohr, Ingrid and Wulfing von, *Die Sieben Heiler*, Fischer, 1992.

Rohr, W., *Meditation: a handbook to western and eastern methods*, Goldmann, Munich, 1991.

Saint-Germain, Comte de, *Studien in Alchemie, Die Wissenschaft der Selbsterfahrung*, Summit Lighthouse, Munich, 1984.

Singh, D., *Spiritual Awakening*, Sawan Kirpal Publications, 1986.

—— *The Wonders of the Inner Worlds*, Sawan Kirpal Publications, 1988.

Books on Dr Bach's flower therapy

(a) Primary literature:

Bach, E., *Heal Thyself*, C. W. Daniel, 1946.

—— *The Twelve Healers and Other Remedies*, C. W. Daniel, 1988.

Wheeler, F. J., *The Bach Remedies Repertory*, C. W. Daniel, 1953.

(b) Other books:

Barnard, J. and M., *The Healing Herbs of Edward Bach. An illustrated Guide to the Flower Remedies*, Flower Remedy Programme, 1988.

Books on colour
Gimbel, T., *Healing Through Colour*, C. W. Daniel, 1987
– a highly sophisticated study of colour in relation to
the various planes of human existence, based on Rudolf
Steiner's work and the author's own researches.
Kraaz, I. S. and Rohr, W. von, *Die Farben Deiner Seele*,
Goldmann 1991, a handbook on colour therapy.
Life Energy Products, *The MultiColor Combi Set for
Chakra-energy, Color Therapy, Color Acupuncture,
Color Meditation and Color Experimentation*, MSI,
Santa Fe, 1989 – the 24-page booklet accompanying
their portable colour lamp.
Sanders, L., *Die Farben Deiner Aura*, Goldmann, 1989 –
a very personal introduction to the subjects of colour,
auras and chakras, together with a chakra colour-
chart.

Books on homoeopathy
Hahnemann, S., *Organon of Medicine*, Gollancz, 1986.
Roy, R., *Homöopathischer Ratgeber für Reisende, beson-
ders für Tropenseisende*, available from Förderverein
Homöopathie, Türkenstr. 63, 8000 München 40,
Germany.
Roy, R. and C., *Selbstheilung durch Homöopathie* – a
comprehensive modern handbook for the application
of homoeopathy.

Books on biochemistry
Hickethier, K., *Lehrbuch der Biochemie* – the basic German reference work for the Schüssler tissue-salts and
their use.*

Books on radiesthesia (research into radiation energies)
Hartman, J. E., *Shamanism for the New Age. A Guide to
Radionics & Radiesthesia*, Aquarian Systems, Placitas,
New Mexico, 1987 – a summary of earlier writers'
discoveries.
Kirchner, G., *Pendel und Wünschelrute. Handbuch der
modernen Radiästhesie*, Ariston, Geneva, 1977 – a
standard work on the various frequencies by which we
are influenced.

*The British equivalent is the Biochemic Handbook *(New Era Laboratories
Ltd.), available from most wholefood and healthfood shops – Tr.*

König, H. L., *Unsichtbare Umwelt*, Moos, 1975.

Tansley, D. V., *Chakras: Rays and Radionics*, C. W. Daniel, 1984 – a sophisticated study of the effects and uses of radiation frequencies.

Westlake, A. T., *The Pattern of Health. A Search for a Greater Understanding of the Life Force in Health and Disease*, Element Books, 1985.

General Index

Index of symptoms

abdomen, dull pressure in left side
    of 105
abrasions 72
acne 55
Adam's apple, nervous spasms of
    49
addiction 50–1
ageing, premature 108
aggression 29, 39, 42, 48, 100
agoraphobia 103
alcohol abuse 90
alcoholism 15, 51
allergies 50
animal bites 69, 81–3
anxiety 19, 46, 73, 37, 92, 100, 118
apathy 52, 87, 104
appetite, lack of 53
arms and legs, involuntary jerking of
    while half-asleep 108
arteries, furred up 98, 108
asthma attacks 69, 91–2
avoidance of contact 87

back, cold 105
backache 40–1, 69
belching, acid 107
biliousness 42
bites 22
bitterness 16
black eye 76
bleeding 44, 69–70, 72–4, 76, 82,
    108
    after accidents 72
    associated with fractures 72
    bright-red 72
    dark-red 83
    from head injuries 73
    internal 72, 74
    menstrual 90

profuse 70, 72
    bright-red 74
prolonged 72
thick, viscous, blackish 102
blisters 79
    transparent, watery 106
blockages 40, 43
    circulatory 49, 73
    emotional 47
    of energy 112
    psychological 111
blocked nose 40, 132
blood, bright-red, spitting or
        coughing up of 74
    dilution 99
    over-activity of 106
    poisoning 70, 82–3, 102
    pressure, falling 72
        high 48–9, 53
        low 52
    prolonged loss of 74
    rapid loss of 74
    severe loss of 90
blue with cold 91–2
blushing 49
bones, weakness of 99
bowels, sluggish 41
breath, rattling 90
    shortness of 72, 92
breathing, difficulty in 81
    problems 83
    shallow 91
        irregular 73
    stopped 79
bronchitis 100
bruises 44, 69, 75–6, 101
burning, feeling of 80
burns 22, 50, 69, 77–9
    degrees of 77
    severe 79